Praise for Professor C

Born to Succeed

Born to Succeed

Releasing Your Business Potential

Colin Turner

'Europe's foremost teacher of business success'
Business Age

TEXERE

New York • London

Original edition published in 1994 by Element Books Limited

This revised edition published in 2002 by

TEXERE LLC
55 East 52nd Street
New York, NY 10055

Tel: +1 (212) 317 5511
Fax: +1 (212) 317 5178
www.etexere.com

In the UK

TEXERE Publishing Limited
71–77 Leadenhall Street
London EC3A 3DE

Tel: +44 (0)20 7204 3644
Fax: +44 (0)20 7208 6701
www.etexere.co.uk

This publication is designed to provide accurate and authoritative
information in regard to the subject matter covered. It is sold with the
understanding that the publisher is not engaged in rendering legal,
accounting, or other professional services. If legal advice or other expert
assistance is required, the services of a competent professional person
should be sought.

Designed and project managed by Macfarlane Production Services, Markyate,
Hertfordshire, England (e-mail: macfarl@aol.com)

Library of Congress Cataloging-in-Publication Data has been applied for

ISBN 1-58799-123-3

Printed in the United States of America

This book is printed on acid-free paper.

10   9   8   7   6   5   4   3   2   1

Contents

The Succeed Trilogy
The Key Stages to Entrepreneurial Success

Over my 30 years in business I have experienced being an apprentice, employee, employer, manager and board director. I have also experienced being an entrepreneur, a partner, a business owner, the leader of an organization and a trainer and consultant. Throughout my career, the research I have undertaken has persistently interacted with my practical business experience in a search to uncover what causes individuals to lack the confidence to succeed while others are confident of success, despite enduring failure; what motivates people to become employees, employers, managers, entrepreneurs and leaders; and what makes certain people achieve, serve, innovate and risk more than colleagues, relatives or partners.

My observations and study have revealed certain insights. The very foundation of personal success is through continuous self-development, though seldom are we aware of the essential tools required for such an important challenge. Similarly the very foundation of business success is through understanding, developing and practising entrepreneurial

characteristics. Indeed every small business and large organization owes its original existence to entrepreneurship.
Furthermore entrepreneurship offers by far the best way to
develop individuals. Confident, self-assured individuals who
are able to align what they do with what they are ensure both
their personal and business success.

The *Succeed* trilogy of books, which I have been
developing and refining over the past eight years, provides
a practical, and I hope inspirational, route-map to follow in
order to harness the potential we all have to find success in
our chosen professions and in our everyday life. The series
begins with *Born to Succeed* which takes the reader on a
journey of self-development and self-awareness with the
aim of providing guidance on how to release their full
potential in business and in life generally. When *Born to
Succeed* was first published, the feedback I received soon
made it clear that the book had inspired many individuals
to set up their own businesses, and many organizations to
take a keener interest in their people. And the simple
message it contained spread far and wide. *Born to Succeed*
was published in some 25 languages and became a No. 1
best-seller in Japan.

The second book in the series, *Paths to Succeed*, guides the
reader in the alignment of their own personal mission with
what they do professionally. It blends eastern philosophy
with contemporary western experience into a practical set of
tools which can be utilized to ensure the reader is best
positioned to maximize success in their career.

Finally, *Lead to Succeed* shows how to develop the ideas
and philosophy captured in the first two books, and apply
them to established and hierarchal organizational structures.
In so doing, *Lead to Succeed* explains how it is possible to
develop and nurture the entrepreneurial leadership attributes

that have become critical within established organizations in order to ensure future growth.

Each book in the series has a specific, self-contained purpose and message and can be read independently of the others. Taken together, all three have been structured to ensure that you, your career and your organization are able to release potential, fulfil purpose and make a worthwhile difference.

Foreword

M any people shy away from studying how to release
one's entrepreneurial potential. Knowing oneself,
believing in oneself, setting goals, mastering one's life and
employing one's purpose all seem, to many, to be 'beyond my
ability'. Why, oh why?

I challenge the doubters to study Colin Turner's persuasive
blueprint for a happier and more fulfilling life. Every day in
my life I meet both the powerful and the meek. There is not
one of them who would not benefit from reading and
absorbing this excellent book. Whether they will, or not, I
cannot say. Sadly, in my experience, the ability to engage in
self-evaluation is an all too rare attribute. Each one of us
should be in love with learning and this desire for self-
improvement should remain with us as long as there is breath
in our body.

Born to Succeed will also I hope fulfil an important
purpose in providing a guide on how to increase the quality
of our present standard of living. Competition with the many
developing industrial countries is a huge challenge and each
one of us, whatever our job, will need to improve our

performance continually if we are to succeed and prosper in the global business environment.

Today one of the 'megatrends' is the move from employment into self-employment. This involves accepting self-responsibility and is very challenging. For people to succeed in their chosen field Part Two, 'Believe in Yourself, Believe in Your Mission' is essential reading.

I sincerely hope millions of people read this inspiring book. When they do they will become more fulfilled and more successful.

As a politician, the sections 'Sweet Are the Uses of Adversity' and 'Obstacles Instruct Not Obstruct' particularly appealed to me. I shall read the book over and over and over again. I hope others will too.

Sir Michael Grylls
Former UK Government Advisor for Entrepreneurship

Part One

The Most Important Living Person This Century

Chapter 1

Created for Achievement

Since the beginning of time mankind has attempted to discover the meaning of life. Philosophers have devoted their lives to revealing the mysteries of our creation:

That which is created must of necessity be created for a cause

remarked Plato, one of the world's great thinkers. The overwhelming conclusion seems to be that: **Our purpose is to realize our potential**. We are given life and our purpose should be to make a success of it – and that success can be measured only by comparing what we actually achieve with what we are potentially able to achieve.

What are we doing about our true potential to achieve? It is waiting to be used, waiting to be activated, waiting to take us to unbelievable heights. Each of us has been created for a purpose, a reason, but if we don't know what it is or what we want, our untapped potential stands idle. Imagine a unique, all-powerful computer whose new operator has lost the instruction manual and therefore cannot make use of the computer's full capacity. If each of us has been created for a specific purpose it follows that everything necessary to achieve that purpose should already be in place. The problem is that we are conditioned not to recognize this purpose. One of the aims of this book is to show how self-imposed limitations have created a barrier to making a success of our lives. First, however, it is necessary to recognize and understand the uniqueness of the most important living person this century ... you.

Unique in the Abundance of Nature

Above the entrance to Socrates' school were the words 'know thyself': recognizing the important fact that you are unique is crucial to this process. The chances of someone else having your biological make-up are in excess of 1 in 50 billion – no one has your fingerprints, your lip prints, your ear or toe prints. Doctors have shown that the composition of your blood is peculiar to you. You are, in fact, a special individual with the capacity to achieve great things. This is because you have the ability to reason and this sets you apart from other forms of life. It has been said that whatever the mind of man can conceive it can achieve.

Most of us seem unable to grasp the fact that we are Nature's crowning glory. There are no restrictions on our potential for or limits to success. Within each individual the potential is there and is waiting to be used. Do you remember at school, for example, thinking: 'How can I do that?' whenever you were instructed to learn a new skill. Yet each time, after pushing yourself, you 'discovered' you had the ability – you even enjoyed it. Once accomplished you never forgot how to ride a bicycle, you had the ability. But you had to really draw on yourself as a child to overcome the inevitable falls.

The secret is that this potential must be called upon. If we feel inadequate in a particular area this is because we have imposed limitations on ourselves. Athletes understand that there is real power in their second wind but they must use their first wind to the full. We simply allow ourselves to block out any available reserve by a refusal to exercise our power of choice. If we don't expect anything, we will consequently not gain anything. If we go to life's fountain with a teaspoon instead of a barrel we are not drawing on our reserves of strength, imagination, vision, insight and creativity together with our own special talents, skills and abilities, and Nature will simply take away what we are not using. In the depths of the ocean there are fish without the need for sight so Nature has removed their eyes. Whatever is not used will atrophy, whatever is used will become stronger – people who work with their hands will find that the blisters turn to callouses and become harder and stronger, and people working with their imagination and creativity will find ideas will flow more easily. Part of this book's aim is to show you how to activate your thought processes – mental muscles – and to draw on your own form of genius.

The 'Genius' Availability

Albert Einstein once said that every child is born a genius. You have the ability to perform at exceptional levels in at least one area of your life if you can find it. It has been proved that the level of intelligence and creativity that you develop is in direct proportion to the quantity and quality of the stimulation that your mind receives. Like any muscle, the more your creative 'muscle' or mind is used the stronger it becomes. Conversely, the less it is stimulated and drawn on, the weaker it becomes. When you study a particular subject, new ideas come to you with your increased understanding. Whenever two or more individuals concentrate together, their minds are stimulated by each other, creating new ideas as a direct result of that stimulation. Reading, more than anything else, stimulates the mind and the imagination. Sadly, the majority of people never read another non-fiction book after they have left school. Reading gets the imagination juices flowing which then in turn flow more quickly with use. The adage of 'use it or lose it' has never been so true when it comes to your innate creativity. Einstein's theory of relativity was born of his imagination, not at the blackboard. While daydreaming he imagined riding on a lightbeam. The degree to which you accept and develop your innate creativity determines how far you go.

From ancient times there has been talk of the human mind being a part of a more powerful mind, the universal subconscious mind, the infinite intelligence, the collective unconscious, the supra-conscious or super-conscious. We all have a super-conscious mind that we use constantly, often in a very disorganized way. Our enthusiasm and excitement, our intuition and insight, our creativity and imagination, and our motivation and inspiration originate in and are controlled by the super-conscious. This wealth of talent is at our fingertips and we have to find ways of drawing on it.

'Genius' is a recognized description of some faculty which is not understood. If asked what is meant by the term 'genius' many people would say it denotes something which is not just thought or emotion, but possibly a blending of the two. Many philosophers, scholars, metaphysicians, poets, writers, scientists, artists and musicians have admitted that they could not explain how their ideas came to them.

The Inner Inheritance

Socrates dramatized his inner voice and called it his daemon which sustained and guided him and preserved his serenity up to the moment of his drinking the hemlock. I am not saying that his philosophical inspiration came only through this voice, but merely that he was influenced by the super-conscious. Describing it in his speech before the court of 501 people he said:

> *Something divine and spiritual comes to me, it is a sort of voice that comes to me ... and when it comes it always holds me back from what I am thinking of doing, but never urges me forward.*

It is interesting how this part of the inner voice, which will be discussed later, tells us which way not to go, never which way to go – it always seems to be a warning voice.

Schopenhauer records that:

> *My philosophies have been produced within me, without my intervention, or those moments where my will was as it were asleep, and my mind was turned in a direction previously determined.*

When Rousseau was describing the sensations he experienced when his first ideas of sociology came to him he said that they came from an intelligence beyond him and that he:

> *felt his head attacked by a giddy stupor like drunkenness.*

The poet Blake said he had written poetry:

> *from immediate dictation, thirty lines at a time, without premeditation and even against my will.*

Beethoven, who was deaf, saw a whole symphony in a flash which then took six weeks to write out. Mozart apparently generated his musical ideas without conscious effort, always note perfect, and in some instances was able to compose music while joining in general conversation and even while listening to the opera. Hoffman described his effort thus:

> *To compose I go to the piano. I shut my eyes and I copy what I hear myself dictate from outside.*

Of Wagner it was written that his work was the expression of a fundamental intuition.

From these observations it could be said that inspiration is another word for a message from the super-conscious part of mind which has contact with a wider world than the conscious mind. Think back; have you ever been driving or walking and an idea comes to you and then some time later, possibly months or years, you have come across the same idea in its physical reality and you will have thought: 'Hey that was my idea'? Of course you have. Because of that experience alone, accept with an open mind that you have an inexhaustible wealth of potential within you in the form of ideas and 'genius' and that you have been born to be exceptional in a particular area in your life. Just imagine if you were able to unlock this power. This book will show you the various ways of doing this.

A Wealth of Opportunity

No one is limited to one chance. Every new day brings a new beginning. Throughout our lives there are new, exciting opportunities but we have to look for them. It is pointless waiting for an opportunity to present itself – this is like standing in the middle of a park, with your hands in the air, waiting for a baseball to drop into them. Opportunity does not chase you, *you* have to go after *it*. Every day on TV and radio and in the newspapers we hear about new discoveries which testify to the talents and abilities of the 'ordinary person' in the worlds of sport, music, literature, technology, medicine, science and the arts. Too many, however, think that those talents exist only in others and not in themselves, yet they are also 'ordinary everyday people'. Every 'ordinary person' is exceptional when involved in the right opportunity, an opportunity of their own creation, making or catching. All too often we miss the boat and someone else grabs the opportunity that should have been ours.

Opportunity is under the iron law of the universe within the dominion of cause and effect. If we fail to look for it we will fail to see it. Those who believe that 'seeing is believing' will live their lives missing one opportunity after another. With a fresh look we can start to recognize the unlimited opportunity that lies all around us. We must learn to see abundance where most see lack. As Marcel Proust said:

> *The real voyage of discovery consists not in seeking new landscapes but in having new eyes.*

There are only three primary colors, red, yellow and blue, but numerous shades have been discovered by artists who saw the potential there. With just seven notes musicians have composed many works and the great poets have not been restricted by only 26 characters in the alphabet. Most opportunities show themselves in the form of a crisis, adversity or failure, and many a success story has started this way. In China the same character is used for opportunity and adversity and yet in the Western world we associate the word failure not with opportunity but with apprehension. Failure is the world's way of providing you with your greatest springboard to success by opening up new opportunities.

A father was shocked on reading his son's school report as it made it plain that the boy was an absolute dunce. The father had hoped that his son would become a barrister but the headmaster made it perfectly clear that there was no possibility of that happening – the boy was a failure.

No, Sir Winston Churchill did not become a barrister – just one of the greatest leaders Great Britain has ever had. Failure projected him towards greatness. Odd though it may seem, failure is often the precursor to success by making you stop and assess your life and look for opportunities. The more times you have failed the better your chance of future success. I will explain why later.

Most Never Exploit Their Abilities

Regardless of your line of work there is always unlimited opportunity and people who can discard conventional disbelief and learn to relate the normally unrelated will not only find all that they want materially but also a great deal of happiness and satisfaction in their achievement. Every human being has sufficient ability, ideas and opportunities to make them rich in every area of their life. Most human beings never exploit their abilities; they choose not to look at the world with new eyes, seeing only the negative instead of the positive.

If you are always waiting for opportunity, making excuse after excuse, you will reach the last excuse of all – 'I'm too old now'. Until the day you die you will feel the world was against you, your genius did not receive the recognition it deserved and those who succeeded did so because of 'luck' or 'influence'. The only difference between a millionaire and you is *you*. You have to be your own worst and most effective enemy. **No power on earth can impede your progress as surely and implacably as you can**. You will only move forward when you understand your unlimited potential and recognize that opportunities are there for you to take as part of your right.

In 1809 there was a baby born in Kentucky whose father was not only poor but also a layabout. The child's mother died when he was nine telling her son that all opportunity had to be looked for not waited for. He was not allowed to read books because his father disapproved. At the age of ten he was able to sleep in a bed for the first time; until then he had had to sleep on the floor. His name was Abraham Lincoln. The statement of 'seek and you will find' means that it is there but you must look for it, it doesn't say wait and it will come.

The following words of Emerson have always meant a great deal to me and I have paraphrased them to share with you:

> So shall we come to look at the world with new eyes. Nature is not fixed but fluid. Spirit alters, moulds, makes it. Every spirit builds itself a house, and beyond its house a world. Know then that the world exists for you. What we are that only can we see. All that Adam had, all that Caesar could do, you have and can do. Adam called his house, heaven and earth; Caesar called his Rome; you perhaps call yours a trade, profession, business or whatever. Yet line for line and point for point your dominion is as great as theirs, though without fine names. Build therefore your own world. As fast as you can conform your life to the pure idea in your mind that will unfold its great proportions.

Your Omnipotent Computer

We have been created with a brain, a biological super-computer that sparkles with the circuitry of a thousand cities. There are more than 10 billion nerve cells in the human cortex, arranged in definite patterns, and it has been suggested that at any given moment there are between 100,000 and 1,000,000 chemical reactions taking place in your brain.

Comparisons have been made between the human brain and one of the world's largest computers – the Cray. For example, that computer even when working at 400 million calculations per second for 100 years would only accomplish what your brain can accomplish in a minute. It is inconceivable that such an incredible network of brilliant intricacy is inside you for the sole purpose of carrying out physical functions. This is the nucleus that has given us space-travel technology, computers, engineering, incredible inventions, the sciences, the arts, and great compositions. It is a transmitting and receiving station that has hatched all we have known, will ever use today and in the future. Do you doubt that this three-and-a-half-pound lump of grey matter that each of us carries around with us can bring you everything you want? Of course it can. You must begin to recognize your power as an individual, that anything you set your mind to work on will become a reality and that anything you don't set your mind on will not. It is simply a matter of choice.

Your brain, which is composed of 10 billion billion working parts, has enough storage capacity to accept ten new facts per second. It has been conservatively estimated that the human brain can store an amount of information equivalent to 100 trillion words, and that all of us use just a minute fraction of this storage space. This is a powerful tool and you could choose to put it to some incredible uses which you have not considered until now. Please keep this in mind as you go through the pages of this book and try to choose new ways of thinking.

Power of Choice

Your power of choice, your ultimate freedom must be your greatest power. You have the power to think whatever you choose to allow into your head. The freedom of choice is your birthright; your circumstances have nothing to do with your destiny, they are merely the result of past choices or non-choice.

Your thoughts are your own, uniquely yours to keep, change, share or contemplate. No one else can get inside your head and experience your own thoughts. You do, indeed, control your thoughts, and your brain is your own to use as you wish. You cannot have a feeling or emotion without first having experienced a thought. Take away your brain and your ability to 'feel' has gone as a feeling is a physical reaction to a thought.

If you can control your thoughts you can determine your feelings and you can choose how you respond or act in a particular situation. This means that you can no longer blame circumstances for any situation you find yourself in. If we can begin to examine our lives in the light of choices we have made or, more significantly, failed to make then we can start to see that we are the person responsible for how we feel. How we have been conditioned to think the way we do will be discussed in the next chapter, but for the moment just accept that you are the sum total of your choices made to date and, therefore, with new choices you can decide to be, have or do anything you want for the future.

Choice Not Consequence

Controlling your thoughts means you are the decider of your fate, in other words you choose what your world will be like. George Bernard Shaw expresses it so well with:

> People are always blaming their circumstances for what they are. I don't believe in circumstances. The people who get on in this world are the people who get up and look for the circumstances they want, and if they can't find them, they make them.

Using your power of choice to make decisions determines your future.

Of course, it is not easy to think in new ways and it requires a great deal of work to unlearn all your old habits. Think back to what seemed to be an insurmountable problem – learning to drive, especially with a manual gearbox. There were three pedals but only two feet and getting to grips with letting out the clutch slowly and pushing down the throttle at the same rate as you released the clutch seemed a real problem when the same foot was needed for the brake. Suddenly, a million mental signals later, no thinking is necessary – driving is just second nature. When did you believe that you could drive? A thought becomes a belief when you've worked on it repeatedly, not when you simply try it once and use your initial inability as the excuse for giving up.

By looking at the characteristics of our power of choice we can see in what ways we can choose our destiny and in understanding them we can increase our belief. In time belief will then add to our understanding and if we know how our choices work we can put them to use.

First, although you do have the freedom in your choice of action you don't have the choice of the consequence. These are always predetermined by the principle of cause and effect where thoughts are causes and conditions are effects. The only way one can make a choice of results or consequence is by making the right choices of actions and attitudes. When you pay for a bad choice you usually pay for it later, but the good that comes to you must be paid for in advance.

Cake and Eat It

Frustration is experienced by wanting to have our cake and eat it; also, by wanting both the pleasures and prestige of one choice and the consequences of another. This is, of course, not possible but many people spend their lives trying to 'beat the system' and when it doesn't work their way they will blame bad luck, fate or someone else for the outcome. But remember you can stay in control by choosing again if the original outcome is not to your liking. For example, if you are following a route and you choose a wrong turn you can choose to make a detour to get back to where you want to go – you don't have to accept that the first road is the one you must stay on, or moreover abort the whole mission. Obviously, it helps if you know where you are going (this will be discussed in a later chapter) but I am amazed at how many people after having made the wrong choice just give up.

Your Own Choice

The choices you make must be your own. Schopenhauer said that:

> *we forfeit three fourths of our lives to be like other people.*

Of course, you should weigh up any consequences your actions may have on others and often it is wise to go and seek the advice and opinion of others. Ultimately the choice is yours because no one else is qualified to make your decisions because they do not have your exact personality and do not have to bear the full consequences of your choice as you must. You must learn to have faith in your own inner guidance system and to develop your power of choice and decision-making by using this.

Use It

Making choices is a talent that must be developed – you are not born with this ability. The more decisions you make the easier it will become to make more and the more you make the better you will become at making them. To make good decisions you must acquire the habit of making choices and with practice you will become mentally prepared for the consequences and able to anticipate them.

Privilege

The power of choice is unique to mankind – it is a privilege – you have the power to choose your environment, your friends, and your thoughts. Only you can open the door to your future and only you can shut it. Making the right choices and doing what you want are what's necessary to make a success of your life.

Of course, it is not true that we can choose right now to end a war, eliminate all crime or cure the sick. We cannot wish away forces previously put in motion by past choices. Circumstances can only be improved by making better choices now or in the future. By the decisions we make and by the attitudes and habits we cultivate we are able to create our own mental, physical, and emotional environment.

Worthwhile Risk

To be able to share freely in all life's opportunities we must exercise the power and privilege of our free choice. If you go down a path that you haven't consciously chosen then you won't achieve your full potential. When we choose we obviously risk losing but we also risk winning. This danger of the unknown makes people delay making a definite choice and they go through life saying: 'Of course, what I should have done,' 'what I could have done,' and 'I wish I had done.'

Procrastination, which will be discussed in a later chapter, is almost the fear of success and certainly the self-imposed obstacle to claiming your birthright and living the life you want for yourself. The infinite resources within you are waiting to be tapped. The atom still exists even though we have never seen one.

We are much more powerful than we choose to believe and this sense of personal power is sometimes difficult to cope with. It is much easier to believe our conditioning which tells us that situations outside affect us inside, that dreams don't come true and that we must accept our lot. You must realize that you can choose and you should choose now. It *must* be better to attempt great things even if sometimes we fail, than to stand on the side-lines of life.

The Success Instinct

Nature has given all living creatures the instinct to survive but she has given *us* another instinct which sets us apart. Mankind has an in-built desire to succeed – something which is as natural to us as breathing. One of our greatest needs is to have a purpose in life and we need this success instinct to achieve this.

So why is it that whereas some people seem to lead an ordinary, uneventful existence others can leave their marks in history and accomplish everything they want. There is little correlation between success and a person's intelligence, education, I.Q., family background, contacts, appearance or even a dynamic personality. Certainly, these factors may have some bearing but they are not enough on their own to guarantee success. Of all the millionaires 80 per cent are self-made. Andrew Carnegie, born in poverty in Scotland, became the world's first commercial billionaire. In the space of a few years William Gates became the richest man in America. Starting with nothing but an idea his 'Microsoft' software is today synonymous with computers yet he and his friends, who are now all financially independent, were considered 'ordinary' at school. Millionaires are ordinary people who set out to achieve extraordinary results. Richard Branson, often referred to as the Peter Pan of the entrepreneurial world, started his music-to-airline empire from a houseboat to become one of the most successful entrepreneurs in the world.

The answer to success is found neither in family heritage nor exceptional I.Q. nor a formal education. Far too many successful people have had none of these advantages. No, success seems to be more a natural consequence of what people are and not a result of what they do or how they act. It has been said that normal health and physical ability are major factors for success but consider the enormous success of Helen Keller who was born deaf and blind. Who would have believed that a cripple could become President of the United States of America but Franklin D. Roosevelt did. Milton, the great poet, who created such vivid images in his *Paradise Lost*, was blind. Who would have believed that a deaf man could compose symphonies if Beethoven had not done just that. Who would believe that great artists and writers could create what they do with either no legs, arms or hardly any ability to move. Stephen Hawking, acclaimed as the new Einstein and whose book, *A Brief History of Time*, was a number one bestseller for over a hundred weeks, is a man so debilitated that he talks through a computer attached to his throat and only has movement in one finger from which he operates everything. Evelyn Glennie is arguably the world's most outstanding solo percussionist, yet she is profoundly deaf. What most people would consider an impediment she says is a musical advantage, a gift. Her lip-reading is brilliant and her voice perfectly modulated. Although she cannot hear the music she feels the vibrations through her feet, legs, hair, scalp and cheekbones. Trevor Jones, an all-round sportsman, was paralyzed from the shoulders down when he broke his neck in a skiing accident. He successfully rebuilt his life, and his achievements include being the first tetraplegic to cross the English Channel in a microlight. One of the most outstanding and positive people I know, Trevor is committed to helping others who are spinally injured. I always remember the incredible Douglas Bader, who lost both his legs in a plane crash before the Second World War. The same thing had happened to hundreds of flyers throughout the world and in every case it finished their flying career. But Douglas Bader became one of the most renowned pilots in one of history's most famous battles – The Battle of Britain. He even led his group and after being captured he managed to escape.

Success may be on an international level or it may be limited to recognition by a small circle of friends or family, but whatever the level the success instinct inspires some to rise above themselves and their circumstances to reach for higher more worthwhile things. Humans are by nature goal-striving and we are not happy unless we are functioning in this way. True success, which has nothing to do with material possessions but is measured by creative accomplishment, and true happiness not only go together but also enhance each other.

So What Exactly is Success?

Success is the continuous accomplishment of planned, meaningful objectives. The majority of people measure their success as compared with others, but genuine success is what people do with their own potential, their development and improvement of it, and must be related to their individual objectives and personal goals. Success, however, does not lie in the achievement of the goal, although that is what the world would have us consider success, instead it lies in the journey towards the goal.

The great thing is not so much where we are, as Oliver Wendell Holmes said, but in what direction we are moving. Success is a journey, it is the result of attitudes and habits acquired on that journey. It is not so much the product of unusual talents and abilities but learning to put those talents and abilities to use. It is not doing the unusual but doing the commonplace unusually well.

Goals and objectives must, therefore, be continually decided upon and set. If you set a series of goals and reach all of them then you must set new higher goals, for if you don't you can no longer be successful. You may have been a success in the past, but if you no longer have a current objective to attain then you cease to be successful by definition. Even if you have decided what your goals are, but do not work towards them, then you are not being successful. Finally, if you have set your goals and you are working towards them but they are not meaningful to you, then you are not being successful.

The important factor to understand is that any development of your potential is meaningful. Success then is related to doing those things which you have not yet done. It is not a comparison with what others have already done. I believe that a major reason for people not achieving what they want is that they do not understand the concept of success.

Success of course is often associated with money and there is absolutely nothing wrong with wealth, money or prosperity when they have been rightfully gained. We in the Western world may have been somewhat conditioned into believing that the accumulation of riches is immoral, but money is neither good nor bad. It is the use to which money is put which is good or bad. Wealth can be a very natural by-product of the successful achievement of a planned, meaningful goal.

Money on its own, however, is a rather unreliable measure of success. For example, when its accumulation is the sole purpose of an individual it cannot be a worthwhile goal because the person will frequently wind up as the slave instead of the master and we do not realize our potential in that way.

Success is more than just the accumulation of wealth. It is also about living a life of daily progress towards goals and service of others because the immutable laws of the universe, to which we are inescapably linked (these will be discussed in a later chapter), ensure that there are rewards. Both Donald Trump and Mother Theresa will go down in history but for different types of achievements.

You and Success

Christopher Morley said:

> *There is only one success, to be able to spend your life in your own way.*

You already possess an unlimited force within you to do this, what is required is the programming of the ultimate computer – your mind. You are the programmer and with the right techniques you can instruct it to select whatever you really want. All the great thinkers have disagreed over many things but they have agreed unanimously on one major truth: we become what we think about.

Solomon said:

> *As a man thinketh in his heart, so is he.*

and Buddha stated that:

> *all that we are is the result of what we have thought.*

Marcus Aurelius wrote:

> *a man's life is what his thoughts make of it.*

and Ralph Waldo Emerson said:

> *a man is what he thinks about all day long.*

So we become what we think about. Each of us becomes exactly what we program our minds to be. A prosperous person programs prosperous thinking into his or her mind and a miserable human being instructs his or her mind to 'make me unhappy, mediocre, boring and average'. Your mind is like soil in a garden – it does not care what you plant – it will always nourish it.

How true the biblical statement:

> *to him who hath, more shall be given and to him who hath not, even that which he hath shall be taken away.*

The rich get richer because they think of what they want and the poor get poorer because they can only think of what they need in order to get by. The universal laws make your dominant thoughts become reality – as Shakespeare said:

> *beware our thoughts lest they betray us.*

and:

> *our doubts are traitors and make us lose the good we oft might win by fearing to attempt.*

Sowing seeds of success with an understanding of the universal laws and proven techniques for activating your inner powerstore, and cultivating them with new pro-grammed habits of action will almost certainly reap a bountiful harvest.

Let's move forward and discover why you think the way you do, why you act in the way you act, and why you will tend to move in a way consistent with what you are familiar with even if it is leading you away from your dreams. Once you know that you can change direction you can reverse the trend and ensure you achieve all that you were created for. Success has no relation to what you are now; it's your power to be the person you can become.

Benjamin Disraeli, author and British Prime Minister, said:

> *I have brought myself by long meditation to the conviction that a human being with a meaningful purpose must accomplish it and that nothing can resist a will that stakes even existence for its fulfilment.*

Let us resolve to find your meaningful purpose, your area of excellence, and the courage and discipline to remove the obstacles that prevent you from attaining your goals.

Make a resolution today to start working on *you* by creating a clear understanding of the infinite potential that exists within you, lying dormant awaiting your activation. Use this book as your guide on an exciting journey of self-discovery. Begin to recognize yourself as someone special with unique talents that you must discover, use and share.

You must make a choice to decide to use your symphony of success which is awaiting your conducting or go to your grave with your music still inside you, unplayed and unheard. Start by making a decision to commit yourself to finishing this book and to understanding and applying the concepts and principles that it conveys – it could change your life, it should, and it will if you choose – after all it's your choice and your life. Now let's go back in time a little and see why we are what we are.

Life can only be understood backwards
it has to be lived forwards.
Kierkegaard

yet

What lies behind us and what lies before us are
tiny matters, compared to what lies within us
Emerson

and

The life which is unexamined is not worth living.
Plato

THOUGHTS FOR SOWING

1. You are the most important living person this century. Believe in the limitless potential within you as your first step to greatness.

2. Whatever your unique talents are you must resolve to discover, use and share them.

3. That which you draw on will increase, that which you share will multiply, that which you withhold will diminish and that which you are born with must be claimed, used and developed.

4. Anyone can be a success if enough doors are opened, all that is required are the keys and they already lie deep within you.

5. Knowledge is *not* a dangerous thing. Ignorance is *not* bliss. Dare to explore the powers of your mind.

Chapter 2

Know Yourself

The helicopter, having just collected its passenger, was leaving the skyscraper landing pad. Strong gusts were making it difficult to take off and inadvertently part of the landing gear had hooked under the support cables of the building's communications satellite. Suddenly, the stressed cable snaps and whiplashes onto the moving rotor blades. Within seconds the crippled flying machine is hanging precariously over the edge of the skyscraper's towering side. Having not had time to buckle up, the passenger is thrown out and Lois Lane finds herself hanging in space clinging to a few electrical leads. One by one the leads break.

Do you remember that part in Superman? It was the first major piece of action in the film and had us all sitting on the edge of our seats – great escapism. As the last lead breaks Lois plummets to what has to be certain death. Stirring music heralds the arrival of the hero. Superman grabs Lois saying: 'Don't worry I've got you'. She frantically replies: 'You've got me, Who's got you!' Some time later, at her apartment Lois asks in a much more familiar way: 'OK Supe. What do you stand for?' Without even blinking an eye he responds: 'Truth, justice and the American way'. Lois, a journalist, almost disbelievingly follows with: 'You're kidding'. To which Superman again replies without hesitation: 'Lois, I never tell a lie'.

Not only does he state his values and what he stands *for*, but he also stands *by* them immediately. Do you know what you stand for? If you were woken up in the middle of the night and asked what you stood for, could you answer? Do you know what you *want* in life? Do you know what *direction* to take?

How important it is to know who we are. Seems like a good starting point, doesn't it? After all, how can you expect to understand others if you don't understand yourself? How can you respect others unless you respect yourself? **The basis of self-respect is self-control and this starts with understanding yourself**.

So who are you? If your name were to be entered in a dictionary how would you define yourself? Just pause for a moment and think about that. Now don't panic and say: 'Oh hell, I don't even know who I am *now*'. Because I can tell you that you *do* know who you are. You can come up with the right answer if you give it some thought. Take a few minutes to write down whatever comes into your head.

Understanding Who You Are

Actions have always spoken louder than words:

> By their fruits you will know them.

the Bible tells us, or to paraphrase Emerson:

> *What you are shouts so loudly at me that I cannot hear you speak.*

We can determine our identities by judging our own actions, but we have to be conscious of what we do and by that I mean being *aware* of what we do. Only by self-study and self-observation can we be made to realize we are unaware. This is not always easy; as Robbie Burns aptly put it:

> *I wish some power the gift would gi'e us, to see ourselves as others see us.*

I remember a man who continually failed to keep not only his appointments with me but also his promises to me. Each and every time we met he moaned about how his business colleagues broke their promises to him and how he prided himself on always keeping his. Amazingly, here was someone, renowned for his unreliability, who saw himself as just the opposite. He was not conscious of his actions and his image of himself was misconceived.

The idea I want to put to you is that mankind, as a species, is not a completed being. Individuals must learn to develop further by their own efforts – if they don't then they lose the capacity for development.

To develop or evolve in this instance means the development of inner qualities. Our individual evolution depends on our understanding of what we can become and what we have to do to achieve this. The truth of the matter is that we must first acquire the qualities which we think we possess, but which we deceive ourselves about.

Self-evaluation enables us to know our limitations and discover our own potential. It is impossible to know ourselves properly without knowing our defects and short-comings. Only by self-evaluation can we establish what we stand for and these values create the basis of our self-concept.

The Self-concept

Our self-concept is like our command center. What we believe about ourselves becomes true as we act in a manner which is consistent with those beliefs. We don't just have one self-concept, however, we have lots of individual ones which come together to make up the complete picture. You, for example, have a self-concept for how you dress, how you speak, behave in public, the kind of parent you are or friend, husband, wife, even driver or lover.

You will react with anger or irritation if someone suggests that you are not the person you think you are – it is challenging your self-concept. Your self-concept will even determine your income level. I have a friend who plays golf regularly. Every time he had an exceptional first nine holes he would say: 'This can't be me, I'm not that good'. Sure enough on the next nine holes his self-concept automatically compensated so that his final score was consistent with what he was familiar with. Self-concept is made up of three critical parts and these are your self-ideal, self-image and self-esteem.

Quite simply the self-ideal is the person you would most like to be. It is your idea of what constitutes a winner. Your self-image is how you see yourself and, most importantly, how you *think* about yourself. It's like an inner mirror, it is how you perceive yourself now and your self-image may still be based upon others' perception of you. Do you know that success begins when you start to reject other people's image of you?

There was a young boy who had lived with his grand-mother since he was just a few years old. He had no self-confidence, it was as though his self-image was destroying him. Other people sensed he had little confidence, in particular the school bully, who beat him more severely than perhaps he should have done. The young boy turned on the bully and knocked him to the ground. The year was about 1670 and this story is not to illustrate why he turned, it is more to show what happened after he turned. Within minutes the boy had a new 'self-image'. Within a few weeks he was head of class and the next term he was head of his school. Years later he was knighted and became Sir Isaac Newton, discoverer of one of the most important universal laws. I say discovered, not invented. The law had always been around and not just in the physical sense that Newton applied it. Its other levels form one of the bases of this book, which with understanding of its principles will make you unstoppable, if applied correctly.

Like Yourself

Your self-esteem, the third part of the self-concept, is how you feel about yourself. It is how much you like yourself as a parent, a boss, an employee, a person. It directly determines your effectiveness in all areas of your life. Fortunately, the self-concept is malleable and therefore the self-esteem can be built. The best definition of self-esteem is how much you like yourself and it can therefore be increased by telling yourself how much you like yourself.

I can almost hear the alarm bells going off in your head as you read that! One of the principal reasons for experiencing difficulty in maintaining a proper self-image and a high self-esteem is that we are taught that self-love is wrong. The origin of this fallacy is probably related to misconceptions of humility and the idea that self-love is related to selfishness. Nothing could be farther from the truth.

As a child you perhaps learned that liking or even loving yourself, which was the most natural thing in the world to do at that time, was being selfish and conceited. Children see themselves as very important little people yet by adulthood all society's well-meaning cautionary messages have firmly taken root. Self-doubt is in full bloom and the reinforcements continue as the years pass. After all what will others think of you if you go around loving yourself!

You must understand the vital role that your self-image plays in the achievement of your success. I am not talking about conceit or a super-inflated ego, I'm talking about a wholesome self-respect – a positive self-image closely related to a recognition of the potential that exists within you. Too many short-circuit their chances for success by having a low self-image, restricting their perception of what they can do by self-imposed limitations caused by conditioning.

Our Conditioned Beliefs

Almost from the moment of our birth we have been conditioned by outside influences. Our parents, family, schools, society and environment have provided well-meaning influences, intended for our own good yet so often resulting in a low self-image. Our natural inheritance, motivation and creativity is thwarted.

Millions of people are diet conscious and we all know the saying 'You are what you eat'. I have said already that all scholars have agreed 'we become what we think about'. It must follow then that the mind is what the mind is fed. Our mind food determines our habits, attitudes and our personalities. Mind food is our environment. Everything that influences our thoughts and the kind of mind food that we have been fed determines how much innate capacity to achieve will develop.

As children we are more often conditioned by influence rather than by some act or experience. When someone remarks that 'the child certainly has his father's temper' it is not because the child inherited it, it is because the child was conditioned to it, he learned it. If we see that a fit of temper results in someone else getting what they want, or getting satisfaction from such a display, we attempt to express ourselves similarly. If it works we continue until it becomes a habit. We then strive to remain consistent with what we are familiar with even if the habit is leading us away from being successful.

Not only by example but also by words, advice, arguments or persuasion our family gives us an idea of what to expect of ourselves. Often these ideas are somewhat limited in scope and a parent who has, for example, been somewhat conditioned to negative responses, can pass on those same attitudes to a child, despite the fact that the child may have far more hidden talents than the parent ever had.

Most of day-to-day conditioning while growing up consists of 'don'ts'. At a surprisingly young age we make plans to conquer the unknown, to be leaders, to do exciting and stimulating things, to become wealthy and famous – to be the greatest. In our imagination we see ourselves achieving it.

'Know Your Place'

Yet before we can reach an age at which we are able to work towards our objectives a multitude of well-meaning but suppressive influences go to work. 'Don't speak until you are spoken to'. 'Don't play in the street'. At school we hear from all sides: 'Know your place' or 'Don't try to be *clever*.' 'Don't *try* to be *clever*'! As teenagers we grow up to hear: 'Don't try to be someone you are not' or '*Who* do you think you are'? 'Who do you *think* you are?' And finally we hear: 'Don't bite off more than you can *chew*!', 'Look before you leap'.

All these help to create the number one obstacle to high-level success which is the feeling that major accomplishment is not for us but for other rather 'lucky' people. This attitude simply stems from a thinking which has been directed towards mediocrity.

To a great extent you are the product of your physical environment and the person you are today, your personality, ambitions, position in life are largely the result of this. The important thing to understand is how you can be and have been conditioned and through such understanding realize that you can use the same methods to reverse the trend. What we can create we can reverse or re-create. If a personality has been shaped by daily exposure to fear, doubt and worry, it can be changed by daily exposure to more positive influences. To be the successful person you have a right to be, you will have to re-condition yourself for success.

We can redesign the way we choose to live, and be the captain of whatever course we choose to plot. Environment shapes us, makes us think the way we do, and assists in forming the beliefs that form our self-concept. Try to name just one habit or mannerism you have which you did not pick up from someone else.

As a child you were born fearless and uninhibited. Your mottoes were 'I can' and 'I don't have to'. During our formative years when we were told 'be careful' and 'no' our mottoes changed to 'I can't' and 'I have to' otherwise known respectively as the fear of failure and the fear of rejection. These conditioned responses manifest themselves when appropriate recognized signals trigger them, creating a barrier to releasing your full potential.

Conditioned Response

Perhaps the most famous exponent of conditioned response was Ivan Petrovich Pavlov, the Russian physiologist. A Nobel Prize winner in 1904 his most widely publicized experiment was with dogs. He rang a bell and then immediately gave the dogs food. At first the dog salivated when they saw the food. Then he found they salivated when he rang the bell before the food was brought. Ultimately the dogs salivated on hearing the 'signal' of the bell sound without being given food at all.

Conditioned response is a very powerful force and in similarity to other forces it can be programmed for good or ill. You have conditioned yourself to respond in the appropriate way to drive a car. Many times you have driven along a route and not had conscious recollection of all the movements you have made. The whole process of driving is a conditioned response. Have you noticed how passengers in your car, who are themselves drivers, will often move their feet involuntarily as something such as another car or animal suddenly crosses your path. It is the controlled automatic response to stimuli.

It is the same with the conditioned responses of your friends and families. Suppose you tell them, with the greatest sincerity that some day you will be the chairman of a large company. What do they say? They probably think you are joking, then when they believe you mean it they start saying things to rationalize their opinions. 'What's the point of all the struggle?' or 'At least you have a good job now' or 'Don't rock the boat' or 'Don't bite off more than you can chew', etc. Yet if you ask a chairman of a large company he won't laugh – he knows it *is* possible as he has *already* done it.

I remember when I first went into business myself I found a superb site on which I intended to develop upmarket housing. It had no planning permission and I had no money but I could see that it could provide the opportunity to build exclusive housing that was in demand in that area. Among the well-meant statements there is one classic that I will never forget. When I first announced I was going to develop sites for luxury housing my father responded with: 'What if the availability of sites dries up?' 'If I were you I would stay where you are'. Within two years the site was developed and is now known as millionaires' row.

New Thinking

You must learn to live your life in a society of compromise without being compromised. You must not be so conditioned that you grow, live, work, marry, retire, and die according to a formula fashioned for you by family, environment or institution. Otherwise you might as well rest under the epitaph: 'Died at twenty, buried at seventy'.

You must condition yourself to expect success from life as the conditions that will divert you are man-made, they are artificial and false. They are the result of limited imagination, yet they melt away whenever you expand your self-image, which you can do by moving into the field of accomplishment. New conditioned beliefs will make you unstoppable. Very simply they are the end product of the right mind food together with repetition. Success is the result of attitudes and attitudes are nothing more than habits of thought. A habit is not an instinct, it is a reaction and a reaction is caused by repetition. In Chapter 4 you will learn how to re-program yourself, meanwhile practice self-observation and start by writing down at least five positive and five negative habits that you have and then write down five habits that you would like to cultivate.

HABIT INVENTORY CHART

	Positive habit	In which way does it help you?
1.		
2.		
3.		
4.		
5.		
	Negative habit	In which way does it hurt you?
1.		
2.		
3.		
4.		
5.		

HABITS TO CULTIVATE

New habit	In which way will it help you?
1.	
2.	
3.	
4.	
5.	

Major Debilitating Devices

With all the conditioning influences surrounding us, it is easy to see how our natural creativity and potential can be severely blocked, or at least diminished. It is these deeply rooted devices that can hold us back from true success. Before creating a plan of action to take you where you want to go it is important to point out the major obstacles that you will encounter and how to overcome them. These are the 'no' syndrome, negative thinking, fear and worry, procrastination, complacency, and past mistakes and failures. Let's take each one in turn.

No! *Syndrome*

Probably more because of parental ignorance than deliberate intent, children are raised in an atmosphere where the typical response is 'no' rather than 'yes'. As the 'no' takes more of a dominant tone the maturing child accepts negatives as a way of life. He or she starts to concentrate on the reason why things can't be done or shouldn't be done, instead of ways they can be obtained, and why they should be accomplished. They are prone to procrastinating and making excuses.

There may have been a time as a child when you wanted to help dad in the garage. 'Can I help dad?', Picking up a tool and wanting to be like dad. 'No', is the reply – 'you might hurt yourself'. A child, of course, does not accept that and continues to ask, or use the tool that he has already picked up, perhaps inadvertently undoing what dad is busy doing and getting in the way at the very least. Eventually in exasperation, the parent says: 'No! no! no! you don't know what you are doing – leave it alone – go and play elsewhere'. The child continues and gets sent to his room.

Years later when dad asks his son to help with something in the garage the now young adult, whose mind still echoes with the well-remembered 'no's' of his childhood, responds with some sort of excuse. He may respond with: 'I am just not good with tools'. All he is doing is acting in a manner consistent with his 'conditioned' self-concept.

Adults who now have a conditioned negative attitude aren't even aware of why they fail to achieve what they want. What they term 'bad luck' seems to confirm their gloomy predictions. They want success and everything the word implies yet they think that failure is due to outside circumstances when all the while they are carrying within themselves the seeds of their own failure – negative thinking.

Negative Thinking

It is important to understand that anyone can unconsciously slip into the habit of thinking negatively. This can be overcome when you view yourself objectively, recognize you are doing it and discover the underlying cause of negative thinking. A negative thought can be replaced by a positive thought using visualization as will be shown later in Chapter 4. For things to change *you* have to change and the key is in building confidence and a belief that you can change yourself and your attitudes. Most change is met with some form of internal resistance. A basic fear of the unknown causes a natural resistance to change and the result is that although we have the desire to have, we don't have the desire to be or become.

Many times clients have said to me: 'If only we had this or that, we could do what we want and then be a market leader'. It doesn't work in that order. *We have to be before we can have.* When we become the person we want, we can do what it takes, to do what we want. Goethe, the German philosopher, said:

Before you can do something, you must become something.

It is the becoming that creates the initial fear as your self-concept will strive to remain consistent with what it is familiar with. This comfort zone throws up all kinds of resistance against change. To overcome fear of change you *must* change; as Mark Twain said:

Do the thing you fear and the death of fear is certain.

Fear and Worry

Fear in itself is good, it is a natural and constructive survival mechanism. When we experience danger physically or psychologically, our built-in alarm system goes off. Adrenalin races and jerks the mind and body to react.

We sometimes subjectively experience a fear, however, without regard for the objective validity of our fear's existence. We react to our conditioned perception of a situation rather than to the actual situation. Some have been conditioned to associate fear with cowardice. It is simply not true to say someone is never afraid, nor is it natural – but we shouldn't be dominated by our fears. As Rudyard Kipling said:

Courage is not the absence of fear, it is the control of fear

the mastery of which can be learned by anyone.

Fear is negative when it is a conditioned response unrelated to any real threat. Prejudices are a form of conditioned fear and these conditioned fears, although they have no basis in fact, can cause us anxiety, distrust and panic. We may have been brought up to believe that all politicians are dishonest, or gypsies steal. Almost all groups of travelers are now termed 'New Age' creating the prejudice that this is another term for a drop out. Yet many pinnacles of 'accepted society' are new-age thinkers and exponents.

Conditioned fears will, if you allow them, frequently divert your attention from more constructive ways of living and achieving. These prejudices or pre-judgements, as we can call them, build up the fear in you which prevents you from exploring the unknown. They certainly prevent you from changing and moving forward and impede your growth. Knowing what you stand for and what you want keeps your attention on a positive path. People who don't know where they stand or where they want to go are, in one sense, inactive and an inactive mind breeds worry which is the most common form of fear.

I remember a statement I read on a calendar over 15 years ago. It read: 'Worry is the interest on the payment not yet due'. It had a profound effect on me because it made me realize the futility of the emotion – a complete waste of time and energy. Most of our present-day living is weighed down by worrying about what might happen in the future. The rest of the time is spent feeling guilty, about what we did in the past. Any spare time left over is used up in worrying about what we should, or shouldn't be doing and feeling guilty about what we could, or couldn't be doing.

There is no time left to live our life to its full potential. Anything we want to do, we have to put off. Next time you find yourself worrying ask yourself: 'What am I putting off by using up this present moment to worry'? Why not make a list of all the things you worried about six months ago. See how many things came to pass and if the worrying was productive. Any future dilemma often turns out to be minor or even a blessing in disguise when it arrives.

Procrastination

Almost everyone who has ever lived has been a procrastinator at some time in their life. Procrastination, or the habit of putting things off, has got to be one of the major factors preventing people from achieving. There are, of course, various degrees of procrastination, yet, in all of them, resolving to do something later which you could do now, becomes an acceptable substitute and a superb expression of self-delusion. The interesting thing about 'later' is that no one can reproach us or prove us false, as when confronted we can say: 'I said I would do it later, it's not later yet'. When you say 'later' to something that is important to you, you are cheating yourself out of your success inheritance.

I have to admit that some of the greatest obstacles to certain planned accomplishments of mine, even to the point of missing opportunities, were self-created by 'putting things off'. A popular reason is using sleep or tiredness as a delaying tactic. Have you noticed how tired you get when you are close to doing something difficult or uncomfortable. Fatigue is a terrific deferring device.

It is crucial to your success that you start putting an end to procrastination *now!*

Do the thing and you will have the power

said Emerson. Just making a start will help you eliminate any anxiety you may have about the project. Procrastination is substituting the now with the anxiety about a future event. If the event becomes now then the anxiety by definition must disappear. How do you tackle situations – take immediate action. Give yourself an allotted time in your diary which you will devote exclusively to the task you have been putting off. The feeling you get is great, you actually find yourself enjoying the task. To quote Goethe again:

Whatever you can do, or dream you can, begin it. Boldness has power, magic and genius in it.

Don't rationalize by saying you have to do it properly. Just completing something by doing it is 100 per cent better than doing well something you never even start. Remember a bad idea acted on is 100 per cent better than a good idea not acted on. Just remember that Winston Churchill spelled perfection as paralysis and look at what he achieved. Perfection means immobility. Change 'do your best' to 'do'. It certainly makes the words of William Blake appropriate:

If you trap the moment before it is ripe
The tears of repentance will certainly wipe

But *if once you let the ripe moment go*
You can never wipe off the tears of woe.

Complacency

Complacency is when we surrender to an inner urge to take it easy. In the same way that most of the tendency to procrastinate comes from not keeping a program of self-evaluation, complacency is self-satisfaction from the belief that there is no point in finding out what you want.

Often a complacent attitude is an indication of a low achievement drive, and people can spend most of their time looking for easy things to do. As the desire to excel doesn't exist, individuals become busy being average, using most of their life distracting others.

I remember at a training seminar I was conducting, I overheard one delegate say to his colleague: 'I need more paper, I have taken loads of notes. Can I borrow some of yours.' The pleasant and complacent colleague responded with 'why knock yourself out? We can't all be successful. Be more like me, I am satisfied just where I am.' I initially thought that the conscientious delegate had been tainted by his colleague's attitude, as there was a lengthy pause. I was mistaken, however, as he replied with: 'Well, as I have even paid for both our tickets I will use your unwanted manual for note-taking – thanks'. Mr Complacent hadn't even paid for his ticket! How many people do you know who want things handed to them on a plate and then don't even bother to make use of them?

Conscientious people cannot afford to wait until they feel like it to make their life's contribution. **Life is not accountable to us, we are accountable to life, and it is up to the individual to decide what that contribution should be**.

Past Mistakes and Failures

No one is born knowing the ways of the world. So it is natural that in our learning process, we will make mistakes and experience failure. Nature's way is to try and fail, to adjust and try again. Birds learn to fly that way and children learn to walk.

When you were small you learned to climb up onto a table or a chair. For some reason you moved one foot in front of the other. You took your first step. What happened next? You fell down banging your head on the table or chair, as you went, and ended up on the floor screaming. What did your parents do? Did they look at you and say: 'Tut, tut, tut, tut, you tried, and you failed! Get that child out of here! No! of course they didn't! They were overjoyed and hugged you and stood you up again! You promptly fell down and when this performance continued you didn't think: 'This is stupid.' Of course, you didn't! You kept on doing it and kept on doing it until eventually you were walking.

Mistakes mark progress. Rough weather builds strong timber. We can either accept a mistake as a failure or as a lesson in progress, as a challenge or as a chastisement. The attitude you develop gradually reconditions you to say: 'I can' or 'It can't be done', before you even try.

No one really enjoys failure. Yet the practice of remembering and re-living past failures is so common that you would think that some people actually enjoy it. The all too human experience of attempting something and failing to accomplish it, should be relatively unimportant. The greatest progress has been achieved through trial and error by people who dared to fail time and time again. Failure becomes significant only when the experience is so strongly entrenched in the memory, that it becomes debilitating to future progress.

At dinner one evening a friend of mine started to discuss his relationship with his ex-fiancée. The relationship had actually ended some three-and-a-half years previously and he was discussing it as if it had only happened yesterday. He told me how it had affected him and also how angry he was that the affair was over. He seemed to be enjoying re-living the past situation so much that I said to him: 'David that was years ago. You must put your experience behind you, learn from it and move forward and start living your life now.' He looked at me aghast and replied to the effect that: 'I've invested over three years feeling bad about that, I'm not going to give it up now!' Invested! Not give it up now! Ask yourself, what are *you* holding onto which is stopping you from moving forward?

They say that public speaking is a fate worse than death, yet our first speech or public performance was done naked, upside down, in a room full of strangers! I have a colleague who, having experienced something as unimportant as forgetting a few lines in a school play, had literally punished herself by re-living this youthful experience vividly, as though it happened yesterday. Time after time after time, she remembers that awful moment when her mind went blank, her school friends laughed and she miserably failed. Over 20 years must have passed since that event but she still refuses to speak in public as each time she vividly recalls her past experience.

Every success is the result of learning. You must learn from the past but you cannot live successfully in it. Don't look backwards unless you plan to go that way. The truth is that there is more to be feared in not making mistakes than in making them. You certainly won't grow and you will see others move forward as *they* face up to the inevitable risk that is inherent in taking the initiative.

The issue at stake is not the failure itself, it is the question of attitude and to develop a healthy attitude towards mistakes and failures, you must see them as an opportunity in life. More importantly you must see them as things that are uniquely your own. You must not deny they are yours. Your struggles and experiences are part of the price you must pay to earn your birthright, and you will be robbed of it if you allow someone else to give you what you should earn for yourself. In the next chapter I will show how major adversity can be harnessed to give you strength. It is your attitude to this that will either strengthen you or weaken you.

The Key Success Determinant

Everything that you do in life is determined by your attitude and almost 90 per cent of your success will be determined by how positive your mental attitude is. We all want good results from life and the most important single factor that guarantees good results is a healthy attitude. Attitude is defined in Webster's dictionary as 'the position or bearing as indicating action, feeling or mood'. In the Oxford dictionary it is defined as a way of thinking. I stated earlier that our thinking determines our actions and it is our actions, feelings and moods that determine the actions, feelings and moods of others.

Remember that attitudes are nothing more than habits of thought and habits can be acquired. They can be formed and learned. Our attitude is something we can control! You see, each of us tends to live up to our expectations, and our expectations about our outcomes form our attitudes. Put simply, your attitude towards life determines life's attitude to you.

What you say and do in life will cause a corresponding effect. So because you get back what you put out, you can determine the quality of your own life. It is significant to note here that you are individually the sum-total of the thinking habits you have acquired up to this point in your life. There is obviously no way of controlling your earlier environmental influences. You can, however, definitely influence your current environment and thoughts. You can consciously and constructively change your habits and attitudes for the better.

To help you evaluate the quality of your attitude in the past, how would you say people have reacted to you when you enter a room. Is it in a smiling, friendly manner?

The World Reflects Back

It is hard to convince people that the world that they experience is merely a reflection of their own attitude. We all know friends and family that take the attitude that if only people would be nice to them, they would be nice in return. Aristotle was so right with his law of expression which states:

Whatever is expressed externally will be impressed internally.

A person with a poor attitude is a magnet for unpleasant experience. They literally attract bad experiences. These experiences act to reinforce the person's poor attitude, by confirming their expectations about poor outcomes.

So attitude is the reflection of the person inside and if we want our world to change for the better then *we* must change first. Remember that the world doesn't care one iota whether you succeed or fail, change for the better or worse. Your attitude to life doesn't affect the world nearly as much as it affects you. How do you develop a good attitude? Quite simply through practice. If you have a poor attitude you will get poor results and if you have a good attitude you will get good results. Why not have a great attitude and get great results!

One of my clients, a large group specializing in information technology, was bemused by certain of their 'intelligent' agents who were getting average results while their 'less intelligent' part-timers were getting fantastic results. On meeting all those concerned it became apparent that the 'less intelligent' as deemed by the company's I.Q. studies, had great attitudes. So my report concluded that a person's attitude was more important than a person's intelligence. The fact that someone is intelligent or not intelligent, educated or not educated makes no difference; the bottom line is that attitudes are more important than facts.

At work and at home practice positive attitudes. Look for the reasons why you can do something, not the reasons why you can't. Develop the 'I'm winning' attitude. Put your intelligence to creative positive use. Use it to find ways to win, not prove you will lose. When you improve your attitude, you automatically improve your capabilities.

Keep practicing self-evaluation, for when you truly understand yourself your attitudes will reflect that understanding. If you want to convey an expression in your eyes, you must think the expression in your mind. You must think: 'I care about you', for your eyes to say: 'I care about you'. You have heard, I am sure, that the eyes are the windows of your soul. No one, absolutely no one, can change the image his or her eyes project without first changing the way he or she thinks.

Attitudes not only show through but they also sound through too. Once while stopping for a late lunch at a really attractive and inviting road-side inn I was greeted with, even before I could say hello, 'too late for last orders' from an assistant, in a manner that portrayed that this person was fed up and wanted to go home. Seconds later another assistant greeted me with 'Good afternoon, sir. Unfortunately the chef has switched off the cookers now, however I can make you a sandwich or a salad if that's alright'. You can imagine that had the second assistant not spoken to me I would not have felt inclined to return to the restaurant let alone recommend it. I wonder how many businesses are destroyed by the attitudes of the front staff. Think of all the planning and energy, not to mention the expense and risk, which is lost forever due to a bad attitude.

The Right Attitude Only Wins

When our attitudes are right our abilities reach a maximum effectiveness and good results inevitably follow. Right attitudes enable you to develop as a leader, they win for you in every situation. Have you noticed how the higher you go in any organization of value, the nicer the people seem to be. Great attitudes naturally gravitate to the top of whatever business or department they are in. They have their positions largely because of their attitudes.

Let me prove my point by giving you an exercise. If you conscientiously follow it you will find yourself becoming 'lucky' as the uninitiated call it. So: treat every person with whom you come in contact as the most important person on earth. Why? Well, as far as every person is concerned he or she is the most important person on earth and by treating everyone this way you will begin to acquire an important habit. There is nothing in the world that people want and need more than self-esteem – the feeling that they are important, they are recognized, needed and respected. They will give their love, respect and business to the person who fills this need.

For the purposes of this exercise act towards others in exactly the same manner as you would want them to act towards you. Treat the members of your family as the very important people they are, the most important in the world. Each morning go out into the world with the kind of attitude you'd have if you were the most successful person on earth. If someone cuts in front of your car, or is rude to you, don't react as they would. Destructive emotions such as jealousy or anger don't hurt others, they hurt you. They can make your life miserable. Forgive everyone that ever hurt you in the past.

Thought Habits

You will find that a great attitude will seem to create unexpected opportunities – a process of happy discoveries, which others refer to as so-called 'lucky breaks'. You will find yourself doing more and doing in less time and you will start to realize that you have placed yourself on the road to what you seek. **Your attitude *will* shape your future**. It is a universal law that works whether your attitude is destructive or constructive. The law states that you will translate into physical reality the thoughts and attitudes which you hold in your mind no matter what they are. Thoughts of poverty are translated into reality just as quickly as thoughts of riches are. Attitudes are habits of thought so keep your mind on what you want and not what you don't want.

Self-acceptance

I mentioned earlier that you have many self-concepts – not a single one, negative or positive. Your self-images are as numerous as your activities and through all of your behavior there is always the person you either accept or reject – you. You exist and self-acceptance means liking the entire you.

Do you like yourself? No real success is possible until a person gains some degree of self-acceptance. Self-acceptance means accepting and coming to terms with yourself now, just as you are. Accepting all your faults, weaknesses, short-comings and inadequacies as well as all your strengths and assets. This is easier if you realize that these negatives belong to you – they are not you.

Just because you have made mistakes does not make you a mistake and just because you have experienced failures doesn't make you a failure. You came into this world to succeed not to fail! Accept yourself for who you are – be yourself! Don't imitate others. Carry your own self-image, not someone else's. Your worth is determined by you and does not require you to justify it to anyone. Just because you may not like your behavior in a given instance it has nothing to do with your self-worth.

Discontented individuals are the ones who are always striving to convince themselves and everyone else that they are something other than they basically are. Success, which comes from self-expression, starts when you are willing to relax and be yourself. Once you accept yourself and choose to be worthy and true to yourself, you can then start improving your self-image. You are better, wiser, stronger and more competent right now than you realize. Creating a better self-image does not create new talents, abilities and powers; it releases and utilizes them.

True self-acceptance means to accept yourself without complaint. To know that to be a human being involves certain human attributes and to accept yourself is therefore the most natural course of action. When you change your self-image, it does not mean changing your *self* or improving your *self*, it means changing your own mental picture, your own estimation, conception and realization of that self. Understand that your 'self' is what you are and always will be. You didn't create it so you cannot change it. What you can do is to realize it. Use your 'self' as the vehicle, as it is the only one you have, for the journey towards self-realization.

Success is a journey not a destination and it is not possible during a lifetime, therefore, for people to fulfil all of their potential. We are necessarily imperfect and therefore always in a state of growth. We can always learn more and therefore perform better. So don't reject yourself for not being perfect, for not necessarily conforming to current fashions of what a person should be or do. Accept yourself as you are.

Take charge of your life by reshaping your self-image. Start by respecting yourself and liking yourself. Get to know the real you. Don't downgrade your abilities, or assets, or dwell on your failures; learn to see yourself as you really are, at your best moments.

Develop a Success Consciousness

Understanding and accepting yourself is tremendously important in success consciousness. A genuine success consciousness does not mean you might succeed, it is a definite promise that you *will* succeed. It is a state of mind in which you cannot see yourself as anything else except a success.

First, know that anything that can be accomplished by someone else can be accomplished by you. There has never been so much opportunity. Of today's millionaires 80 per cent made it in the last 20 years. Of all the scientists that have ever lived 90 per cent are alive today. More literature and information has become available in the last ten years than in the last

4,000 years. Fortunes in every area of life are made in people's minds. You have to believe things before you see things.

YOUR FIVE CHIEF QUALITIES

1.	
Name	Name
2.	
Name	Name
3.	
Name	Name
4.	
Name	Name
5.	
Name	Name

Take the time to determine your five chief qualities. Are you hard working, thoughtful, disciplined, punctual, interested in people, etc.? Enrol the help of an objective friend who will give you an honest opinion, possibly your spouse, colleague or teacher, etc. Under each quality or asset write the names of two people that you know who have achieved substantial success, but who do not have this asset or quality to as great a degree as you do. You will find that you out-rank many successful people on at least one quality or asset. You will find that people who have already accomplished what you want to accomplish, are no different. One day they decided to do it.

Develop an 'I will' attitude and an 'I can' awareness. There is nothing better to enhance your self-respect and improve your self-image. Remember, it is starting a task that requires more effort than continuing once the task is under way, and developing a state of mind of 'I can' and 'I will' builds the self-confidence to be able to start it.

Believing is Seeing

Quite a common expression is 'I'll believe it when I see it'. You can say to someone that something works and it is still not enough. Before it is accepted certain people must analyze it, dissect it, pull it to pieces and tear it apart. They have no belief unless they can be made to see how it works. Once they know this, they will believe, although sometimes even seeing is not enough. Believing is seeing and we only see what we believe, and until we believe we can have something, we won't see it.

Once you believe something you increase your awareness of what you are looking for and you attract the things in harmony with your belief which you overlooked before. To take a simple analogy, you decide to buy another car, something a bit different that you haven't noticed before, but something which fits in with what you want. In driving it home you suddenly notice lots of similar cars, even close by where you live. The power to attract is within you and you must be forever conscious that you possess it. There must be a conscious awareness and you must be able to generate it to create, not to repel.

Imagine that we all send out different strengths of vibration depending on the size of our thoughts. You live in a world where it is accepted that radar and radio waves are constantly around us and will pass through any solid object. Yet only a few generations ago Marconi, who developed a successful method of radio telegraphy, was put in a strait-jacket for his ideas. The fact is that regardless of when they were discovered, radio waves and vibrational waves are always and have always been in the atmosphere. Marconi simply found a way of harnessing them to create a form of communication. The metaphysical details are beyond the scope of this book and may form the basis of a future book – but to give you a clearer idea of thoughts, let us toss a pebble into a pond. You will see ripples or small waves. They spread out in circles and ultimately reach the shore where they appear to stop. Two stones of different sizes and weights, tossed in simultaneously at different places, both send out ripples or waves converging on each other, and where the two stones' ripples meet there appears to be a struggle as to which is to overcome the other. The ripples from the larger stone sweep over the ripples from the smaller stone and create waves in the wake of the small ripples. And so it is with your thoughts – the bigger your thought and the more forceful and vital it is, the more likely it is to sweep over all the smaller thoughts and win through. When we send out a thought in our electromagnetic world in which we live, it sets up waves, and a positive thought is much bigger, has a quicker tempo, and a far greater vibration.

Your positive thoughts will sweep all others aside as you plunge them into this ocean of vibration and electricity. They will sweep over everything to reach their objective, because positive thoughts are like the bigger pebble, they have the biggest wave.

The human mind is constantly attracting vibrations which harmonize with its dominant thoughts. So when you believe, you see the reality. The universal law of belief states that what you really believe in with feeling will become your reality.

It is already a well-known fact that whatever one repeats to oneself, either true or false, one will eventually believe. If it is a lie it will be accepted as the truth. Everyone is what they are, because of the dominating thoughts which occupy their minds.

Faith is a state of mind which can be induced or created by constantly repeating something. It transforms the ordinary vibrations of thought in a powerful and unstoppable process of bringing about the reality you want. Believe that the 'I'm positive, I can' attitude generates the power, skill and energy to succeed. When you believe the 'I *can* do it', and really believe, the how to do it automatically develops and you see the results.

It is essential that through self-understanding, self-acceptance and planning your life, you encourage the positive emotions to be the dominating thoughts in your mind and, of course, discourage and eliminate negative emotions. When you believe an attitude is strong and positive, you will actually seem to control your conditions and make circumstances work for you, not against you. Your belief is one of the most precious things you have, so don't let people with little or no belief try to lead you astray. If you listen to them you will be living their life and not yours. The majority of people do not put much faith in belief, which is why only a small percentage of each generation fully lives the life they have chosen for themselves. As Frank Lloyd Wright said:

> The thing always happens that you really believe in, and the belief in the thing makes it happen

usually long before you see it.

We do not see things as they are,
we see them as we are.

The Talmud

yet

He who looks outside dreams,
who looks inside wakes.

C. G. Jung

and

If you understand, things are
just the way they are;
If you do not understand, things
are just the way they are.

Zen koan

THOUGHTS FOR SOWING

1. If you don't understand or accept yourself, how can you expect others to understand or accept you.

2. Your past doesn't equal your future unless you choose to allow it to by keeping it alive.

3. If you don't make mistakes you are not growing. Learn and keep moving forward.

4. Your attitude is more important than intelligence or facts.

5. You can do it when you believe you can, only then will you see you are right.

Part Two

Believe in Yourself:
Believe in Your Mission

Chapter 3

What Do You Really Want?

The Power Within You

Whatever you believe with feeling becomes your reality. You have the power within you to make your world, your reality, just what you want it to be. Every human being wants success, yet the majority of every generation don't even give themselves a chance because they believe that whatever they undertake, will *not* turn out how they want it to. Disbelief certainly goes hand in hand with failure to achieve.

So many people don't even know what they want and they *believe* that they have to accept their lives as they are. Those who *do* have an inclination of what they want, *believe* they won't achieve it or *believe* they don't deserve it. The key ingredient for success is really believing and true success starts with believing in yourself.

Remember the biblical quotation that faith can move mountains? Well you have to really believe that you can move a 'mountain', whatever it may be, before you can. In the early 1980s I was invited to China and Hong Kong by a colleague of mine who was an engineer involved in the building of the

Hong Kong and Shanghai Bank, at that time the most expensive single construction project in the world. From leading Tai-pans, I learned the true philosophy of moving mountains. I was shown a mountain, mostly of granite, and was enthusiastically informed the mountain was to be moved to make way for new housing. The man telling me had absolute belief and determination in his eyes. Remember the how to do it *always* comes to the person who believes they can do it.

Just ten months later back in Hong Kong on business I took another trip to see the mountain. It was gone! Where the mountain had stood were the foundations of new buildings. Where the sea had met the mountain was now extended to provide a small harbor.

Believing in yourself must never be confused with wishing for yourself. You can't wish away a mountain or wish yourself in a better position. But you can move a 'mountain' or secure the life you want with beliefs. The biblical quotation of *all* things being possible to the person who believes is the most practical wisdom that exists.

Because of self-doubt created by questioning your abilities it is easier to believe that things are not all possible. If no one told you any different you would believe you could. It has been proved that aerodynamically the bumble bee can't fly but no one has told the bumble bee. Yan Chow arrived in Hong Kong an impoverished, emaciated 18-year-old Vietnamese boat person. He was told he could 'be a millionaire'. When I met him he was 25 and a millionaire. He told me that it was not until he was 25 that he had learnt that he had misinterpreted the dialect from 'could' to '*would*' be a millionaire. He believed it and no one told him anything to the contrary.

Wishing is Not Believing

Every day in every location there are young people starting a new career. They all wish that someday they will get what they want, whatever that is, and reach the top. They never do, however, because the disbelief they carry with them creates a barrier, hiding from view the path which becomes visible only with beliefs.

Their attitude is that of the 'average' person. Yet this practice of self-condemnation is so ridiculous – half the population is above average. A small percentage of every generation, however, really believe they will succeed and with that belief they are able to reach the top. When they define exactly what they want they become unstoppable. **The very fact you are reading this book puts you in that percentage of people who can achieve whatever they believe**. Belief can carry you far. It can make you do the seemingly impossible. So often the stumbling block, however, is not knowing what you want.

To quote Viktor Frankl's book *Man's Search for Meaning*:

Everyone has their own specific vocation or mission in life to carry out a concrete assignment which demands fulfilment. Therein they cannot be replaced, nor can their life be repeated. Thus everyone's task is as unique as is their opportunity to implement it.

The only question is, are you going to fulfil your earthly destiny or will you, as the majority does, go to your grave with your music still in you, simply being unable to conduct your own symphony of success by not believing you can be what you want, do what you want and have what you want?

It is one of the most important questions of your life. Are you going to fulfil your potential and become everything you are capable of becoming? Most people do not. By self-evaluation you will have started to establish your values – or what is important to you. What you want and the goals you set to achieve what you want, is underlined by a values system. Establishing values beforehand influences the choices that you will have to make in life.

Before moving on, if you are having difficulty in knowing what you stand for, use this exercise. Spend a good hour on your own and write down everything that you feel is important to you. Don't concern yourself, evaluate or judge what you write down at this stage. Put down anything in any area that comes to mind as you write, from career to health, from holidays to family, cars, education, friends, integrity, reputation. Now this is hard work, but you will find that as the ink starts to flow your thoughts will start to flow. Keep asking what it is that you stand for and let your heart guide you. Writing helps crystallize your thinking to assist you in knowing where and what you stand for now and where you are going. As the measure of your success will inevitably depend on how well you are able to answer these questions, keep on writing until you have about 80 items listed. No matter how insignificant something looks, initially, still put it down. Next, after a short break go back to your list and cut it down to 40 items. Then cut it down again, this time to 20 items. Then to ten and finally to five. These five items can form the basis of your value system. With practice and self-study you will begin to attune yourself to what is important to you, which of your beliefs are the strongest and what thoughts carry the deepest conviction and manifest themselves in your actions. Remember, just do it, as Anthony De Mello said:

People who deliberate fully before they take a step will spend their lives on one leg.

So now, what do you *really* want? You have got to know what it is you want! Picasso's words: 'Man's greatest seduction is his work' are meaningless until you are doing exactly what you want. If your vocation becomes your vacation, you never have to 'work' again as you will be doing what you have chosen for yourself.

Sometimes the only way to find what it is you want to do is to go ahead and do something. Then the moment you start to act, your feelings become clear. Yet the question you want to ask yourself is best stated by Dr Robert Schuller and is:

What would you attempt to do if you knew you could not fail?

What would you dare to do if you knew success was guaranteed? The greatest craving is for meaning and purpose in life and when you have worthy goals based on what you really want, which are consistent with your values, there is a most satisfying feeling stemming from an inherent realization that you are becoming what you want to be.

Your Work Must Absorb You

Everyone has an area of excellence in which he or she can excel. This area has to be first discovered by asking some simple questions for which *you* already hold the answers. D. H. Lawrence said that:

There is no point in work unless it absorbs you, like an absorbing game. If it doesn't absorb you, if it is never any fun, don't do it.

So what really absorbs you? What activity do you sometimes do that absorbs you so much that you lose track of time?

Next, what holds your interest? What holds your interest *so much* that your mind doesn't wander, that you are able to concentrate on it, almost without conscious effort? Next what holds your attention or commands your attention, pulling you away from other subjects? What interests you and holds your attention as you are driving and listening to the radio? What books catch your eye? What snippets of information or conversation spark your interest?

Put simply, what you *love* to do is a sign from your inner guidance of what you *are* to do. You see, the direction our inner guidance shows us will frighten us by reversing our usual or conditioned logic, yet nothing is impossible when we follow it.

Let me give you some more questions to start the reflective process going. What would you do if you won the jackpot in the lottery right now? In other words you can do anything you want – you have complete freedom to choose. Would you stay in the same job? The same relationship? How about hobbies? Would you start a business? Would you sell your business and open a restaurant with you as the chef? Would you give lectures on your subject? Would you write a book? Would you make your hobby or absorbing interest your new career because you can put more time into it?

What is your answer to these questions? If your answer to changing your job is *yes* then you are probably in the wrong job now. The important thing to understand is anything you decide to *be* or to *do*, you *can*. It may not happen as quickly as it would if you already had the winnings, but it would still happen if you really wanted it.

What would you do if you suddenly found out you only had six months to live? Would you carry on doing what you are doing now? What would you want to accomplish? The truth is that not many of us will ever know that we have only six months to live.

The other truth is how much do you really want it? Are you willing to pay the price, whatever it is for doing what you want? Don't allow rational thinking to get in the way of your life's dream.

Now please don't misunderstand me. Everyone has certain commitments and responsibilities in life, of course, but so often these are used as the reason for not living the life you truly want for yourself. The more you are willing to trust yourself, take risks and follow your inner guidance, do what you 'feel' you want not what you *ought* or *should* as delineated by others, and the more, of whatever it is you want, you will have. As Shakti Gawain says:

> *the universe will pay you to be yourself and do what you really love.*

Do you think when you die your Maker is going to ask: 'Why didn't you do that or this?' or 'why didn't you become or discover such and such?' No, the only question asked in that precious moment will be 'Why didn't you become *you*?'

Keep coming back to this section regularly until you are able to recognize those activities that really absorb you and remember to think on paper.

Why Haven't You Already Got It?

A probing question to assist you in defining what you want is: 'If these are the really important things you want to be in life, do in life or have, why do you not already have them'?

This is not meant to be sarcastic; it is meant to get you to reflect as you will find that the answers you come up with are often a list of external circumstances.

To take charge of your life involves accepting self-responsibility. Accepting that everything you are or ever will be is completely up to you and you alone. It is unfortunate although very usual, however, not to know this and be conditioned, as we have discussed, not to believe it. Most people live by the law of accident which simply states if you fail to plan, you are planning to fail.

Why is it people don't get what they want? And why is it that when people do decide what they want they don't ever get it? What are the reasons? And why is it that so many procrastinate all their lives until it is too late? They usually have a dozen reasons why they don't achieve. I have listed the 'true dozen' for non-achievement.

1. No Goals

Many people do not know what goals are, or their vital importance as an ingredient towards achieving what they want. People either write lists before they go shopping, or they are persuaded to spend more money than they intended. We plan our holidays, or we experience boredom. Goals are objectives, aims, intentions. They are not a wish, they are a vivid dream acted on. Imagine a game of soccer without goals.

Others choose not to make goals because of the embarrassment incurred in not reaching them, or what people might think, or whether people will laugh. To overcome the fear of rejection is simple – keep them private and confidential. It is the only way, incidentally, that you can be perfectly honest with yourself. So often we make goals just to impress others: there is a 'me I think I am' and a 'me I want others to think I am'. Therefore we tend to distort our goals and wants in a way that fits an image of how another person sees us.

Goals must be those things *you* really want to become and want to have, *not* a list of objectives you have made up to impress other people. Some people have no goals because they do not have time to set goals almost to the point, for example, that they are so busy earning money they haven't got time to make money. Others are afraid and create the cry of 'I can't'. Failure is essential to success as I will discuss in more depth later.

2. Not Clearly and Specifically Defined

The goals you set for yourself are a prelude to action, they are not a wish or a substitute for reality and as such must provide a clear course to take. You cannot 'drift' from one destination to another. It is not much good to study for this and prepare for that if your destination is not clear and specific. It would be like going to France with a road map of the UK.

Say you want money. How much? £100? €30,000? $1 million? As I write I see someone outside. I bet they have got money. Maybe loose change in their pocket. When you say you want money is that what you mean? If it were a town how would you possibly find it on a map or find a road leading to it? No, wanting money is much too vague a concept; it is like saying I want to go somewhere in the US. You must be specific.

Vague notions such as 'I want to be a success' or 'I would like to be famous' mean absolutely nothing. They are just slightly more specific than saying: 'I want something'. Say, for example, you want to be a musician. That is pretty unclear. Do you mean writing music, conducting music or playing music? What kind of music? In a band, group or orchestra?

When you were at school you may have held a magnifying glass near a piece of paper until the sun shining through it became a pin-point like a laser beam. What happened? It caught fire. You won't catch fire until you clearly define what your goals are and focus on them. The enthusiasm which will be kindled will burn brightly with a specific goal.

3. No Reasons Why

Very often people aren't short of goals but they are short of reasons why they want to achieve their goals. Desire is perhaps the starting point of all great achievement. It is necessary, therefore, to develop a deep down *burning* desire and also know how to generate it, in order to draw on your latent strength and power.

I believe it is important to know what creates desire as it seems to provide the critical ingredients that differentiates between the champion and the person who finishes a split second later. When we set down all our reasons for becoming, doing or having, we effectively list all the benefits to gain or the losses to be avoided. When we concentrate on them, our imagination stimulates our emotional appetite, and the result is the release of strong emotions we call desire.

If there are no reasons for why you want a goal, if there are no benefits or rewards, then you have an empty goal. A goal must make you excited and if there are no reasons to get excited then you have not stated your goal properly. Also by asking yourself why you want a goal you question your motives and this assists in eliminating all those goals for which there is no specific reason for obtaining them. For them to work, goals must have a significant importance to you.

4. Impatience

We all tend to suffer from the expediency factor. We do things that are fast and easy and shy away from that which is difficult and time-consuming. Establishing wants and goals in a defined fashion is hard work. It requires concentrated effort and often at times hours or days to refine. Yet it does become easier as you keep practicing. And you will start finding that your life becomes incredibly easier. So in the long run patience saves time. I am not talking about 'everything comes to him who waits' as that would be nonsense in this context. That is the very reason some goals are never achieved, in the hope that your ship will come in one day. You have to plan and prepare, so that when you recognize the opportunity that is consistent with your want, you are ready for it. With no goal how will you recognize it?

5. Unrealistic Expectations

It follows that due to impatience we tend to set goals that have unrealistic expectations. Not only in outcomes but also in the time factor. The level of thinking that got you where you are today is not necessarily the level of thinking that will take you where you want to go tomorrow.

When we discover what we want, we want it now. We base our expectations on previous experience, or more dangerously on others' experience and when we don't get the outcomes or deadlines we anticipated, because they were unrealistic, we abort the whole mission with the comment: 'that always happens to me – I won't bother to waste my time again'. That is like driving from one city to another to collect something. Half way there you have to make a detour because of road works. Later you break down. Do you abort the whole mission? No, you make contact and say you have been delayed. Never be a slave to a deadline, always be a master to one. A goal without a deadline is not a goal it is a delusion, but sometimes you have to make adjustments for unforeseen setbacks.

Be sure to set yourself realistic goals. Once you have achieved this set another higher goal. If you want to be a concert pianist don't book the hall or venue, book the piano lessons. If you want to earn an income of $150,000 per annum and you are earning $15,000 per annum at the moment then make a plan to increase your income by 25 per cent a year. When you have done *that* you can do it again. In ten years time you will have reached your goal. Who knows you may have to re-adjust the deadline to five years?

Don't confuse realistic with unchallenging. Goals must involve a challenge yet be believable and achievable. They should have a 50/50 probability of success and should be set at the next step on the ladder to your final achievement.

6. Fear of Change

All growth, however, involves some form of change and therefore for things to change one must appropriately initiate change in oneself. It is because of the unknown, of course, that change is scary. Yet whenever, or as soon as, it becomes goal-directed, it no longer becomes something to avoid. The key to your success is to control the direction of change.

Sometimes, client companies of mine have resisted change on the basis that they have always done it this way or more classically: 'If it is not broken, why fix it'. The past doesn't equal the future, however, and the way we perceive the world is more often than not in a blinkered way. The fact remains that if the 'promise' of the better future was there, there would be no resistance to change. The way to control your future and direct your change is to have written goals. The instant this is done the fear of change starts to dissipate as we become accustomed to goal-directed change. It is important to understand that to move forward change cannot be avoided, and it is important to understand that each change provides an opportunity for an innovation, and a chance to demonstrate your own skills or creativity which you will find starts to flow more as change stimulates it.

7. Not Written Down

The ancient pharaohs used to say: 'so let it be written, so let it be done'. Writing crystallizes thought and thought motivates action.

The very fact of putting your goals down on paper creates a psychological commitment. It allows you also to set your priorities, set deadlines and get the balance right. Writing also highlights any conflicts between your goals and values as well as serving as a measure of your progress. Writing them down also provides a guide to help you stay on course. Writing them down stimulates your imagination in the form of visualizing the outcome of your goals. This in turn increases your creativity to assist you in a successful completion of what you decide.

Reviewing your goals can only be done if they are written down. If you went to your doctor and he or she listened to you but didn't make notes and then the next time you went you had to go through it all again, what sort of impression would you get? Remember the weakest of ink is better than the strongest of memories.

8. No Commitment

Commitment is not something that you can manufacture, it is something that you discover deep down inside you. Until there is commitment there will always be a way back or a way to avoid doing what is essential to your goals and achievements. The instant you commit yourself to something is the instant you start achieving it.

9. No Plan

When I was building luxury one-off housing and elegant office blocks I always ensured that I had the best plans. They were very detailed even down to the various shapes of bricks for windows, number and positions of the power points in the kitchen and the shrubs in the garden. Now I am no master builder, but I knew what I wanted. I visualized it and had the plans produced. Give me the best, most gifted master builder in the world and he would not be able to build anything if I didn't let him have a plan. You *must* have a plan. No ifs, no buts, no excuses. Without a plan you will never achieve what you are potentially capable of.

Conviction is, of course, a much stronger ingredient for success than method. But a plan helps you solidify your foundation which in turn provides a springboard to your goals, while measuring your growth. To have a plan is the same as having a blueprint for your success. In the next chapter there is a format for a plan for you to copy and utilize for yourself.

10. No Reward System

When people set goals they tend to move with gritted teeth and determination: 'I am going to do this if it kills me'. Yes, of course, determination is important, particularly in your resolve to achieve what you have set out, but a rigid type of determination can be self-defeating.

You should have a reward system for all your small, medium and big goals. It doesn't matter how little the reward is, as long as there is a reward. For example, if by following your goal your plan involves making say ten phone calls a day, each time you make a call, pass one paper clip from one side of your desk to the other. It sounds ridiculous doesn't it! It works though so who cares! When you have passed all ten clips over this achievement gets you a cup of coffee, a five-minute break, a glass of wine in the evening – it doesn't matter. What does matter is that it makes the path towards your desired goal fun.

Each success is put into your memory until being a success becomes a habit. If you wait for a major positive result as a sign you are on the way, you could start losing your motivation for doing it anyway. A reward system format is also set out in the next chapter.

11. Can't See It

If only more directed use of the power of imagination were made, there would be more success stories. Nothing can be materially accomplished without being mentally accomplished first. The importance of visualization, or seeing yourself as if you have already achieved your goal, cannot be overstated. More about this in depth later, but understand that not visualizing is a major reason for non-attainment of goals and not getting what you want.

12. No Action

Although this is self-explanatory it wins the award for so many not living the life they want. What ever it is – *do it!* Your written plan with its schedule of priorities will tell you what you have to do so don't cheat yourself, do it! Make that phone call. Write that letter. Meet or arrange to meet with the people that can assist you. If you have to learn a new skill – learn it. If it means reading more – take a speed-reading course. If it means doing something that you haven't done before, do it. Do whatever it takes!

You have nothing to lose and everything to gain. No matter how good your goal or your plan is and no matter how much you visualize it, if you are not prepared to take positive action towards your objective, then you are just fooling yourself.

Who are the fools, the people who don't know they have the ability yet use it or the people who have the ability but refuse to use it? Remember wherever there is a demand for an ability the supply will be found when demanded. The secret of the successful person is that it is demanded.

'Sweet Are the Uses of Adversity'

So said Shakespeare. He didn't mean adversity itself was sweet, but that nature almost seems to use it in a way that results in a positive outcome. Napoleon Hill, the author of the classic *Think and Grow Rich*, said:

> For every adversity there is the seed of an equivalent or greater benefit.

How often has something happened in the past which seemed like a disaster at the time but later turned out to be a blessing in disguise.

There is wisdom in the Chinese language as they have the same symbols for the words crisis and opportunity. It is not until something drastic happens that we are forced out of our comfort zone or safe harbor and made to look at our life in a different way.

Strangely enough the greater the crisis, the greater seems to be the opportunity. The majority of millionaires have gone broke more than twice and end up making a fortune, sometimes in a completely different field.

I remember a television report several years ago which was about a venture capital organization in the US which specialized in lending money to people who had been broke once before on the basis that they had experienced the necessary learning curve and were now a safe bet.

Everyone must cut their teeth on some form of experience. It is not the crisis or adversity that is the problem, it's the way you react to it which is the problem.

So often we waste time and energy in blaming why we are in a situation and how 'we don't deserve this'. Instead we should be using the time to learn, re-group and move again, and we should be using our energy to be creative in raising a phoenix from the ashes of our crisis.

Depressions and recessions are man-made and wreak havoc in the same way as nature's storms and gales. Sometimes it is nature's pruning method.

During one of the worst gales in the UK this century when millions upon millions of trees were uprooted, a business colleague was killed by a falling tree. 'What is the advantage in that?' you ask. I don't know. I wasn't involved in that event, and I am not the creator or taker of lives. I believe there were very few people in the country at that time who were not affected by that gale and items were on the news some weeks afterwards. The important thing is how individuals reacted to their own personal events. Whether good or bad comes from it depends on how the individual interprets the crisis. The comments from individuals ranged from: 'what can I learn from this?', 'what can I do about it?', 'how can I turn it round?' and 'what preventative measures can we take to stop it happening again? to the other types of comments: 'why did this happen to me?', 'who is to blame?' 'who is going to pay for it?' 'who is going to sort it out for me?' and 'it isn't fair' and 'why did "they" allow this to happen?' I remember that the weather man was the most hated person in the country at the time. I also remember having several misfortunes that day, one of which was an old English walnut tree which had blown down in the garden. The seed of benefit for myself was that this was a potentially dangerous tree, it needed to come down yet I was unable to touch it as it had been protected. When it fell I made a few phone calls that day and sold the timber to a specialist carpenter who required high-class walnut for his veneering work.

In common with many I have experienced great adversity and each time you learn how to respond and with each response you learn a stronger character – if you choose to learn from it. I believe that for every battle won or lost you emerge stronger, for there is no other way to build character.

I could never concentrate at school and left with few qualifications. With belief in myself, goals and a plan I went from earning £1,000 a year to be worth several million in ten years. Obviously, there were adversities on the way and I learned from these, but then I lost everything.

The fact that my major lending source went down, was declared insolvent, and pulled me with them, is irrelevant. I took responsibility because I had to. You have to look for the solution, not whom to blame. I went, with my family, from a Victorian mansion to a one-bedroomed cottage next to a work-shop. What was the benefit I learned? It taught me more about myself than the building of the company had done. I was right back where I started in a one-bedroomed cottage sitting on a bed settee with a telephone and a writing pad, only this time with a family. The difference was I knew I had done it before so I knew I could do it again, and with the learning experience I had I started to look at how I could turn it all around. Now I worked hard but if hard work was the only prerequisite for success then the majority of the population would be wealthy, but adversity stimulates the imagination, stimulates creativity and you start looking for opportunities within that adversity. I made my plan around that and within three years was in an even better position than before. It then happened again!

Security?

This time it was called a recession, but I still took responsibility personally which helped me look for a benefit and a solution. I didn't spend my time blaming the government. How can a country blame someone they have already chosen to govern for them? There is no security, there is only opportunity. A man and woman can work for the whole of their lifetime with only three words between security and insecurity, between employment and unemployment: 'You're fired' or 'you're redundant' or 'I'm sorry'. Civilizations don't have futures. Countries don't have futures. Companies don't have futures. It is the people that form the companies, the countries and the civilizations that have futures. Civilizations can grow, plateau and fall off. Civilizations can last a thousand years and still fall off, companies can last a hundred years and still fall. It is only you and you as an individual that has a future and whatever future that is, it is entirely up to you. The only security is in the soul of the individual, and that security is found in the belief in yourself whenever you meet an adversity or a crisis that knocks you back. It is the security in the hunger and desire to create meaning and purpose in your life. It is having the security to leave your mark.

The second time I couldn't believe it had happened. And this time it was worse. Rather than keep pushing against something that would not appear to be changed, despite the usual cries of 'something must happen soon', I made something happen. I changed direction, made a new plan, learned new skills and within 12 months I turned over £1 million in a completely different business. More importantly the change in direction made me focus on what I really wanted to do.

The interesting thing is that this completely new business was the one thing that had always absorbed me, always interested me and always held my attention. My vocation is now my vacation and the work I do is a labor of love, which is extremely satisfying and fulfilling. Now if it had not been for my adversity I would never have been granted that opportunity.

Everyone has stories similar to this, I use mine because the only true way to explain something of this nature is to use your own experience. You may not see the benefits of a crisis until some time after, but if you look for it and believe it, you will see it. To quote Virginia Satir:

> *Life is not the way it is supposed to be, it is the way it is. The way you cope with it makes the difference.*

The first noble truth of Buddha is: life is difficult. Well, as soon as you accept that, it becomes easy!

Obstacles Instruct Not Obstruct

If you could so order your life as to avoid all types of adversity, how could you develop character? Adversity mustn't be avoided or feared, it must be embraced and overcome. Persistence is to the character of man or woman as carbon is to steel. It tempers it and makes you stronger. Every time something happens say to yourself, 'what can I learn from this? What benefit can I derive from this? What opportunities have been shown to me?'

There is a story I would like to tell you about a young man who dreamed about being a farmer. He found a farm and bought it. He was not very experienced in business matters, he just wanted to grow crops and cereals, but after completing his purchase he found insufficient water to irrigate his produce.

Following the source of a river he came across a huge boulder which had fallen in the path of the river and had diverted the flow to the rocks where it was lost. He resolved to smash this obstacle to his dreams and immediately went to get a sledgehammer. He hit the rock once with all his strength. Nothing happened. Not even a mark. Not even a splinter of rock. It was as if he had not even hit it. He hit it again and again and again, for over 500 times he kept hitting it. There was still nothing and he started to question his resolve. He started to doubt whether he could move it. He began to question whether he should have bought the farm. He began to doubt if he should have been a farmer. And if you question *anything* long enough you start to doubt it.

After a short break he hit it again and the 502nd time the rock cleaved right into two and the water gushed through. What did it? The 502nd hit or the 502 hits? You see, you don't always get what you want or desire straightaway. You have to keep chipping away, chipping away until you win through. So many stop when they have almost succeeded. What really had done it was the farmer's resolve, which although he questioned and began to doubt, he stuck to his original commitment. That obstacle instructed him more than it had obstructed him. To be a success you have to believe in yourself, and you have to do what you must do when you should do it, and keep on doing it till you win through.

You have to commit yourself to keep going not when it is easy but when it is *tough*. When the going is really tough. When everything inside you is telling you to give up. For me the poem of R. W. Service sums it up so well:

And so in the strife of the battle of life,
It's easy to fight when you're winning;
It's easy to slave, and starve, and be brave,
When the dawn of success is beginning.
But the man who can meet despair and defeat
With a cheer, there's the man of God's choosing;
The man who can fight to Heaven's own height
Is the man who can fight when he's losing.

Make a decision that you will never give up. Look upon setbacks as lessons that you must endure before you can become what you want.

Don't let self-created obstacles or self-doubt defeat you before you start. Resolve to keep going until you win through! It won't kill you and what doesn't kill you makes you stronger. In the words of Polly Berends:

Everything that happens to you is your teacher. The secret is
to learn to sit at the feet of your own life and be taught by it.
Everything that happens is either a blessing which is also a
lesson, or a lesson which is also a blessing.

Restoring the Character Ethic

So often we pick up 'quick fix' techniques to improve our personality. To get to a certain standing, status or social station we learn ways to get other people, who could be important to us, to like us. Although not initially intended as such, these various personality methods or approaches become manipulative, and deceptive – designed for the individual to get what they want from people, or to get where they want to go, as quickly as possible.

Take the scenario of two business people meeting for the first time in preparation to negotiate a deal. One or both may give or receive the 'power look', which I like to call the serious stare technique. This form of expression or intimidation can only work in the short term as it can have the façade of falseness. Why? Because instinctively we read each other's body language. What the individual is trying to convey is that 'I'm strong, I'm confident, I'm important'. To act sincerely towards another you must feel sincerely towards another. How? By working on your depth of character. Eye contact, which is important, will then allow your genuineness to show through. There is then not the necessity to externally cover internal securities with 'personality clothes'. All things being equal you can sense insincerity a mile off, but if two people engaged in conversation have perhaps both been exposed to these type of techniques, then they may not even be aware of it. As Bacon said:

> *For behaviour, men learn it as they take diseases, one of another.*

People communicate not by what they say but how they feel about what they say. What I have realized more than anything else in speaking at seminars or lectures was that it was what I was feeling that was communicated to the audience, more than the words. Words make up only about seven per cent of communication, so shallow personality techniques are registered by an individual even if it is 'just a feeling about someone'.

I have said that the way to build character is to learn from our lessons in life. Only in the crucible of experience can a depth of character be strengthened. As Emerson said in his essay on experience:

Life is a succession of lessons which must be lived to be understood.

A basis of solid values is an incredibly important ingredient in determining how we react or how we respond to our lessons in life. Many commandments, convictions and philosophies are deemed by various schools of thought to be unrelated or not appropriate for the various ideologies. There is one, however, which they all agree on – a golden rule: **Do unto others as you would have others do unto you**.

Stemming from this are the virtues which form the foundation of success – true success – such as: integrity, sincerity, humility, courage, justice and modesty. By interpreting these kinds of principles and habits into our basic character in effect restores the character ethic in all areas of our lives. We as human beings have basic needs which we strive to satisfy at a lower level before we tend to consider these needs at a higher level. Our basic biological needs, water and food, are our lower-order needs rising to the desire to be secure physically and psychologically. Above these is the need to be loved and accepted by others and the need to enhance one's self-esteem. Finally, at the top is our desire to develop to our full potential and to become the best person we can be, with the fullest range of skills and talents we are capable of developing. All of us have the capacity to attain this state. Again to quote Emerson:

> As soon as the first wants are satisfied, the higher wants become imperative.

Yet we must acquire habits or the virtues as a means towards that end.

You Acquire Strength Not Borrow It

We cannot borrow strength as borrowing strength creates weakness. We must acquire strength. Character cannot be made except by a steady, long, continued process. In reading biographies of true individuals such as Franklin or Johnson, Carnegie or Boswell, to name a few, I noticed one similarity. When desiring to improve qualities, which they felt were latent or indeed acquire new qualities for character improvement, they each chose one at a time. They picked that virtue which they felt was the most important to them and mastered it, until it was habitual, before moving on to the next.

As an exercise concentrate on a virtue or a principle that you wish to acquire or improve, each day for a week. You have already detailed certain qualities in the last chapter. Pick one and respond by proper action every time the occasion arises. If you want to improve your sincerity, for example, act towards others in a way that you would want to be acted towards. Use no hurtful deceit, think innocently and justly, and if you speak, accordingly. Ask yourself: 'Is this how a sincere person would speak?' Remember, think it in your heart before you speak. If you speak what is not in your heart then the conflicts you will feel will actually fatigue you.

Using human influence tactics to get others to do what you want them to do while your character has the fundamental flow of insincerity, will certainly not lead to success. Restoring the character ethic by self-understanding and acceptance, generally working on your self and learning from adversity, is the key to fulfilling your potential and acquiring the success that you are capable of. This coupled with established goals and a plan, will ensure an enriched life of enduring happiness.

An Inviolable Plan

We will now formulate a plan for mastering your life but first, I want to share with you the 'inviolable plan' of James Boswell written to himself on 16 October 1763 which I have segmented from the original:

> You have got an excellent heart and bright parts. For some years past you have been idle, dissipated, absurd and unhappy. Let those years be thought of no more. You are now determined to form yourself into a man. You have been long without a fixed plan and have felt the misery of being unsettled. You are to attain habits of study, so that you may have constant entertainment by yourself, nor be at the mercy of every company; and to attain propriety of conduct that you may be respected. You must act as you feel you should do in the general tenor of life and that will establish your character.
>
> Remember that idleness renders you quite unhappy. Let this be no more. Let your mind be filled with nobler principles. Remember the dignity of human nature. Remember that everything may be endured.
>
> Without a real plan, life is insipid and uneasy. Have constant command of yourself. Restrain ludicrous talents and by habit talk always on some useful subjects, or enliven

conversation with moderate cheerfulness. Keep to study ever to improve. Have your own plan and don't be put out of it. Never talk of yourself, nor repeat what you hear in a company. Be firm and persist like a philosopher.

Now remember what you have resolved. Keep firm to your plan. Life has much uneasiness; that is certain. Always remember that, and it will never surprise you. Remember also life has much happiness. To bear is the noble power of man. This gives true dignity.

You have a character to support. Every man should be the best judge of how to regulate his own conduct; there are many minutiae particular to every character. What may be innocent to others is a fault to you till you attain more command of yourself.

Know thyself; reverence thyself; but at the same time be afraid for thyself. Ever keep in mind your firm resolutions. If you should at times forget them, don't be cast down. Return with double vigour to the field of propriety. Upon the whole you will be an excellent character. You have all the advantages from the approbation of the world, in your rational plan, which may be enlarged as you see occasion. But yield not to whims, nor ever be rash.

A musician must make music
An artist must paint
A poet must write
If he is to ultimately
Be at peace with himself
Abraham Maslow

and

One must have chaos in ones self
In order to give birth to a dancing star.
Friedrich Nietzsche

so

Instead of seeing the rug being pulled from under us
We can learn to dance on a shifting carpet.

Thomas Crum

THOUGHTS FOR SOWING

1. Out of crisis there is an opportunity to be found.

2. How you react to change created by adversity will determine your success or failure.

3. Look upon every obstacle as part payment towards your success. Use them to strengthen you not to weaken you.

4. Spend more time on your life list than you do on your shopping list.

5. You cannot be distracted from what you want, when you are absorbed with what you do.

6. If one's motives are wrong nothing can be right.

7. What would you dare to do if you knew it was impossible to fail?

Chapter 4

Mastering Your Life

There comes a point in everyone's life when it is time to make a special decision. Everybody feels the time, yet so many swallow, ignore their feelings and continue putting up with life the way it is. They may feel a little more guilt or, its flipside, resentment or even regret. Whatever the emotion, it manifests itself every so often in the sadness of what might have been if only ...

It can happen when you are a teenager, when you are 20, 30, 40, 50, 60, or even 70. I know one gentleman who made this special decision when he was 78! 'Better late than not at all', when it comes to a life decision, has got to be preferred.

The decision comes from the self-realization of: 'if it's to be, it's up to me'. Halley's comet comes once in a lifetime, the planets align themselves a few times a millennium, and there comes a rare time in the spirit of the individual when all the emotions are channeled in one thought and the heart and mind shouts in unison: enough! At that moment your determination, your desire, and your resolve fill you with a form of energy which, if channeled correctly, makes you a very powerful force.

It may be prior to self-understanding, self-acceptance or increase in self-esteem and self-confidence, or it may be after it. It will have been brought about by a complete realization that only through self-responsibility will you be master of your own life. This acknowledgement brings all the other emotions of empowerment together. Then with a formulated plan of action and the ability to pay the price, you go from achievement to achievement.

This chapter is also like a workshop. In it you will find formats of plans and reward charts. By following the instructions faithfully you will create the basis of a blueprint for your life. Life is not an audition, you only get one chance to play the part you want. Use the guides to establish your foundations. With practice it will become a habit which will be part of a second nature.

If you are to be more successful in your outside world you have to work to control your inside world. Only then will you see your outside world change, and quickly. Those people experience frustration because they attempt to change their outside world. Let's take an automobile for an analogy.

You have the world's most beautiful car. You polish the outside until it really shines. That car's 'self-image' is going to be terrific. Inside, however, the engine is never cared for. That car's 'self-esteem', the starting point of performance, is pretty third rate. The fuel you put in the tank equates to the goals allowing it to move forward, if the carburetor, its desire, injects it properly to allow all the cylinders of emotion to work in the right order.

The handbrake is its fears and doubts which must be released. The four wheels comprise of ... yes but; what if; blame and anger. With any wheel locked on the car goes round in circles even at full speed. The brake and accelerator are the car's logic and emotion respectively, ensuring smooth progress each time the gear of confidence moves up. The steering wheel is the car's choice of direction, it can go wherever it's directed. And the clutch is the car's self-responsibility. Only by letting the clutch out will it move forward. The clutch causes movement, assuming responsibility for all other factors. Even with the brake off and the engine full on the clutch has control. The map, with its highlighted directions, is on the passenger seat awaiting, with the car, the key of the individual.

Do you remember your first driving lesson? Do you remember when you first raised that clutch or depressed the accelerator? When you first took responsibility of that car, when your foot made it move? You probably moved all over the place. It is the same when you accept responsibility for your life – it isn't smooth at first. Later, a million signals later, you changed gear and drove smoothly, without thinking about it. It is the same with self-responsibility. You will inevitably enjoy the smoothness of mastering your life, of being in control of *you*!

No Free Lunch

The price you will have to pay for your success has to be paid in full and has to be paid in advance, so it is important to identify and pay the price. On the road to claiming this success you want there is 'no free lunch'. You have to make sacrifices, whether in the form of pleasure time, or else studying new skills, or tightening the belt while saving for something, but by identifying the price, you can decide if you are willing to pay it.

When you have calculated what the cost is to you, compare it to the major benefits you will receive from achieving your goal and you will see just how small the price is. As you will see, the formats I have laid out highlight benefits and rewards – generally the reasons why. My reason for this is that experience has shown me that many people do not even dare to dream about being successful because of the fear of paying a price. As it is easier to be more negative at a planning stage, the thought of having to pay a price of any kind is so daunting that the enthusiasm for achieving ambitions or goals can be diminished. Knowing the price ensures you prepare yourself physiologically and psychologically in terms of resolve and discipline, in the same way you prepare yourself to pick up a barbell or a newspaper. (Think of the times you have picked up an empty kettle that you thought was full!). When you focus on the expected benefits the price is put into proportion and becomes acceptable – assuming you have decided it is worth it to you (I will cover this later). Remember, however, that the price for achieving poor results is much greater than that for achieving extraordinary results. Remember *you* are responsible for you.

Everything Counts

In setting goals it is important to understand that everything counts. Once you start along the path of what you want everything you do will either move you towards it or move you away from it. As you are responsible for all of your own actions, anything you do, or don't do, will be cheating yourself, surely the highest form of self-irresponsibility. The majority of adults watch between 20 and 30 hours of television a week and then convince themselves that they haven't got time to do what they want. They delude themselves: 'why shouldn't I? It's the only way I can relax and I've been working all day long and deserve it'. What happens is that another evening spent taking them another small step towards what they want has gone. The rationalization is usually 'last night doesn't count'. **Everything counts! Everything that takes you towards what you want is right and everything that moves you away from what you want is wrong.** If it has formed part of your reward system then it is built into your plan. If not, then perhaps what you thought you wanted, you don't really want after all. You must increase the reasons why to generate your desire. Desire, when harnessed is sheer power. Failure to follow desire, to do what you want to do most, paves the way to mediocrity.

One to two hours a day every day will take you where you want to go in the same way many steps make a long journey. Each step is a positive count. Each stop is a negative count. Neutral does not exist. Keep you mind on what you want and not on what you don't want.

Programming Yourself to Succeed

When you program a choice through the steering wheel of your 'life vehicle', which we discussed above, it turns either left or right at your touch. Your map or plan has shown you the correct route to go. Now is the time to get right down to formalizing a plan – a personal plan for you. Over the years I have seen many goal-setting plans and techniques, often incorporating wads of paper and cards. A plan must be simple, easy to fill out and have all the information you require at a glance.

Following is the format of a plan which I want you to enlarge when copying. You will need a master copy, as in the early days you will be utilizing numerous copies for each area of your life. While following this instruction please do the same for the reward contract chart.

GOAL:					
Type:	**Area:**				

Why wanted:
1.
2.
3.
4.
5.

Major benefit:

Obstacles	**Solutions**
1.	
2.	
3.	
4.	
5.	

PLAN

Action stepping stones	Date Expt	Date Achd	Hour Price	Result (F.G.E.)	Reward Recvd
1.					
2.					
3.					
4.					
5.					

Overall target date:

Affirmation 1 :
Affirmation 2 :

Commitment :

Date .... Signed ....

GOAL: To weigh 175 lb	
Type: Medium Range	**Area:** Physical/Health

Why wanted:
1. To look good, feel good and feel sexy
2. To enjoy more health and energy
3. To feel more confident
4. To be better at golf, tennis, swimming, etc.
5. To make my clothes fit me

Major benefit: To increase my self-esteem

Obstacles	**Solutions**
1. 20 lb overweight	Cut down/follow diet/take advice
2. No spare time	Do only 10 mins exercise each day
3. Love my food	Use treats as rewards – cut down
4. Hate exercise	Do what I enjoy – walk and swim
5. Spouse is good cook	Enrol their support

PLAN

Action stepping stones Present weight is 195 lb	Date Expt	Date Achd	Hour Price	Result (F.G.E.)	Reward Recvd
1. Reduce 4lb to 191lb. Join club, schedule swimming	1 April	25 March	hr	E	✓
2. 4lb more to 187lb. Keep on diet – cut out sugar	1 May	2 May	hr	G	✓
3. 4lb more to 183lb. Exercise twice per week	June	June	1 hr	G	✓
4. 4lb more to 179lb. Play tennis – less chocolate	1 July	7 July	1 hr	F	✓
5. 4lb more to 175lb. Keep up exercise	21 Aug	20 Aug	1 hr	E	✓
Great: Clothes altered and not so breathless anymore!					

Overall target date:

Affirmation 1 : I WEIGH 175 LB
Affirmation 2 : I ENJOY GOOD HEALTH AND ENERGY

Commitment : I promise to follow this plan faithfully making any adjustments necessary until I achieve my Goal

Date ....2 March.......... **Signed** .......I.M. Somebody.........

Goals, Types and Areas

You will now have an understanding of how unique you are, of the infinite opportunity available and your power to do something about it. You will have started to recognize your positive qualities and your negative emotions and how you have been programmed or conditioned to think, feel and act up to this moment. You will have started being aware of what you stand for, what's important to you and what holds your interest and absorbs you. Goals are the catapult which project you to your chosen dream.

Goals can be short, medium or long range. They can be tangible and intangible. They will cover all the areas of your life. Remember, however, that you must set goals of becoming – of developing whatever personality characteristics you lack before you reach the more tangible goals of having. Understand that your willingness to recognize the need for and to work toward internal changes is one of the most essential factors of goal-setting.

1. Goal

To define the goals which are important to you and which will be used on your plan, make a list of everything you have ever wanted or dreamed of. Whatever it is, write it down. Give no thought at this stage how you can afford it or how you will ever achieve it. This 'wants' list will broaden your horizon. You must not even try to work out how you will ever satisfy them. There is good reason for this as each time you try to work out how, you will constrict and limit your beliefs in your ability to achieve them. They're currently too far off in the distance and as your planning will be limited to what you know about yourself now, you will write yourself off.

Why list them then you say? If they are really important to you, you will start to see opportunities which you overlooked before. You will unconsciously begin to gravitate towards them. You will begin to develop the abilities to take you to them. So list everything that comes to your mind. Desire means 'of the father'. In other words you would not have the desire unless you had the God-given ability to achieve them. Your values will help you organize and prioritize later.

Sometimes you will not achieve a goal in just the way you plan it. Often the trail of creative planning and action leads you in directions that you had not anticipated, often even greater and even more successful than those in your plan. As I have said, your level of thinking which has determined where you are today will change as you grow.

As well as listing all your wants, also list certain tangible needs you will require in order to make the necessary enhancements to achieve certain goals. For example, if you need to study more in any area to increase your income and there is simply no more time available, make it a goal to take a speed-reading class or memory and concentration course so you are able to do more in less time. It's not the hours you put in, it's what you put in the hours that counts.

List all your intangible wants. There will be certain character traits you will want to develop in order for you to become what you want. For example, if you are intolerant, impatient or short with people, list your goals of improving your understanding of and empathy with others. You may find that these goals are difficult to reduce to writing. The important thing to remember is that these lists don't have to be shown to anyone else, not your friends, boss, parents; and parts at least not even to your spouse. You have to be completely honest with yourself about yourself. Don't let goals, particularly intangible goals, be distorted because you feel you may show them or they may be seen by others. It is your life. They are your goals. Be honest.

When we look to 'others' for direction in what we personally want to become, do or have, we abandon one of our greatest talents – the ability to plan, imagine and prescribe for ourselves.

2. Types

When you have finished your lists organize them in short, medium or long-range goals. Short should be any time period from 1 day to 3 months. Medium should be up to 12 months and long term from 1 to 3 years. Any goals formed after this will form life plans and purpose which I will cover later. The important thing is to learn the art of goal-setting, to enjoy it, make it a habit and watch yourself grow in confidence and happiness. Although they must be challenging, remember that they must be realistic. What is short term for one person may be long term for another. For example, two people may both have a goal to weigh 175 pounds. If one of them is 230 pounds he or she may spread that weight over a period of 20 months. Another may only have to lose 12 pounds and may spread it over 3 months. For the first to lose all the weight in 3 months is completely unrealistic and self-defeating. For the second to lose the weight in 20 months is completely unchallenging and will produce procrastination and complacency. He or she will know that it would only be necessary to lose a few ounces in the first month so may not even bother to start! Unchallenging goals are not goals at all.

3. Areas

Organize them into the areas that make up your life. Balance is important (I will cover this later), but for now just categorize what you have listed. Now this listing is important and please do it. The best time is to write down everything you can think of this evening and then in the morning when you are fresh, get up an hour earlier (just this once for the moment!) and add to your list, organize it into types and categorize into areas. You will find that the evening work will get the thought processes ready for the morning. Say to yourself last thing 'I want to know what I really want to become, to do, and have'. Go to sleep thinking of all the things that excite you (in *all* areas of your life please!). When you wake go to a desk and write – don't write in bed at this stage. It's too important. If you don't have enough time then carry on in the evening.

To get your mind going I have listed sample goals and categorized them into the six key areas of your life.

SAMPLE GOAL LIST

Financial/Career
- Buy a house next year
- Double your earnings
- Buy a motor-boat
- Become financially independent
- Start your own business
- Get a promotion
- Open a restaurant
- Pay for college
- Buy an Aston Martin
- Become chairman of your company
- Get involved in a career you really want

Physical/Health
- Work out three times a week
- Lose 15lb in weight

- Eat more healthily
- Join a health club
- Run a marathon
- Take part in the Olympics
- Give up smoking

Family/Social

- Find a good partner
- Spend 'quality' time with family
- Take a week-end off with your spouse
- Join a new club and make new friends
- Book a family holiday
- Organize a party
- Get married

Personal/Fun/Adventure

- Learn another language
- Climb a mountain
- Take a speed-reading course
- Get a pet dog or cat
- Travel around the world
- Write a play
- Learn to water-ski
- Take a degree
- Fly a plane
- Take an art class
- Appear in a Hollywood movie

Mental/Emotional

- Learn to relax
- Stop procrastinating
- Become more tolerant and patient

- Increase your concentration
- Become more creative
- Be more honest in your relationships
- Become more motivated and positive
- Be more disciplined with yourself

Spiritual/Ethical
- Forgive yourself
- Forgive those who have wronged you
- Treat others with integrity, compassion and understanding
- Develop a personal relationship with God, the universal mind, the creator, infinite intelligence, the universe

When you have organized your list pick twelve items from the whole list. Ideally there should be three from each area but in practice there is usually more from one area than another. Don't worry at this stage about that and keep the goal list handy so you can keep adding to it as you think of other things. Either invest in a large format hardback type for your goal journal to keep everything in one place, or create a specific file on your computer. As you practice, become more competent and increase your understanding and knowledge of your wants, likes and dislikes, it is interesting to see the change in focus from one item to another. You may discover that things you inadvertently listed become important to you, while others seemingly important lose their appeal. As you grow your perceptions will change and your beliefs and values will become more clearly defined. Your goals will underline your value system and highlight any conflicts. You will become more aware of being aware.

4. Why Wanted

Next transpose your chosen items onto your goal and plan sheet, put in the types and areas in the appropriate boxes. Now, to me the most important part, list the reasons why. You should list at least five reasons why you want the goal, and the more reasons you list the more your emotional desires will be generated. If you can list 50 then that is absolutely fantastic and you are already on your way to getting it. If you cannot list more than two ask yourself if you really want it. Perhaps you want it for someone else, or because you think it may impress. Whether it's bungee jumping, speaking Japanese or racing cars, you must really want it for *you* and have good reasons for wanting it. When you become more competent at goal-setting you'll be able to set goals which will involve others and benefit others too. At this stage, however, it is more important to build up your own personal belief system in you, your confidence in you. By attaining lots of successes you will achieve this.

So often people will do or undertake something to achieve someone else's goals. I remember a friend married because his parents' goal was to become grandparents, as well as have the daughter (in-law) they never had. The girls' parents had similar goals. As both individuals had been 'conditioned' to put their parents first they consented – after all they got on well. Unfortunately, it didn't last six months and on that occasion their respective parents didn't get their grandchild.

Live your life, not the life someone else wants for you. They may have chosen their dreams, loves, goals and ambitions and they may not have. Whatever, their outcome is a result of their previously made decisions. Don't let missed dreams be made into your dreams. For a dream to work it must be yours. I love the words of Khalil Gibran in his beautiful book *The Prophet*, from which I reproduce a part:

Your children are not your children.
They are the sons and daughters of Life's longing for itself.
They come through you but not from you,
And though they are with you, yet they belong not to you.
You may give them your love but not your thoughts, for they
have their own thoughts.
You may house their bodies but not their souls,
For their souls dwell in the house of tomorrow, which you
cannot visit, not even in your dreams.
You may strive to be like them, but seek not to make them like
you.
For life goes not backward nor tarries with yesterday.
You are the bows from which your children as living arrows
are sent forth.
The archer sees the mark upon the path of the infinite and He
bends you with His might that His arrows may go swift and far.

If you have a thread attached to an arrow, it will never go its full distance whatever that may be. Honor your parents, love them, but live your own life. You were born to succeed. Whatever dreams and goals you have, move towards them with reasons that come from your heart and don't do something because it only appears rational to do so. If you have children or when and if you do, guide them, advise them but never forget your dreams are yours, let theirs be theirs:

Let your bending in the Archer's hand be for gladness;
For even as he loves the arrow that flies, so He loves also the
bow that is stable.

5. Major Benefit

List here the benefit that will excite you, that will really truly give you a sense of satisfaction, confidence, well-being. This and all the whys will provide the enthusiasm and energy to enable you to cope with all the obstacles you will meet on the way to attaining your goals.

Nothing great will ever be achieved without enthusiasm

said Ralph Waldo Emerson. Enthusiasm is the most wonderfully contagious commodity. It has the wonderful capacity to grow the more you share it. The Latin words 'enthos' and 'theos' that make up the word, mean 'within' and 'spirit', respectively. So enthusiasm actually means 'spirit within'. Your enthusiasm can only stem from your excitement about what you are doing. Those people who look as if they have been weaned on a pickled onion do what they do by rote, by conditioned habit. The movers of the world behave because of their enthusiasm. Make certain your reasons why and your major benefit make you excited. If you're not excited, no matter how you show it (you know when you're excited), then you have stated your goal incorrectly.

6. Obstacles

Under this heading on your plan write down all those things preventing you from reaching your goal. Only by writing down the reasons why you don't have it now will it crystallize your thinking and cause you to start thinking of the solutions. Amazingly enough you will find that you actually know what to do to resolve a problem, certainly solutions will come to you which you had not entertained before. Why? Because the problem has never been defined before and as long as the reason and benefits are greater, the obstacles can be overcome. Remember that anyone who has accomplished already what you want to accomplish had also to overcome their own obstacles. It is only your 'comfort zone' which will throw up an internal resistance of: 'I won't be able to do that'. If no solutions come to you straightaway keep focusing on what you want, not what you don't want and the solution will come.

Learn from the philosophy of the ant which the Hong Kong inhabitants have taken for their own. When your mind is made up an obstacle doesn't even exist. You go round it, over it, under it, or through it, but you keep going forward! You will see from the example Goal Plan Sheet that against each obstacle I have put a solution. If you need more paper for some of your goals – which you will – then use it.

7. Solution

As I have said, knowing the nature of the problem goes a long way to solving it. You have to diagnose before you prescribe. It is almost uncanny the way the answer comes to you, and it is always introspective; you find the solution within yourself.

8. Plan – Stepping Stones

Here you will find there is space for action steps, their expected date of fruition, actual date achieved, price in hours paid, the result, fair, good or excellent and reward received. Break your goals down into smaller chunks. If you want to increase your reading rate from 200 to 800 words per minute with better retention then chunk it down to steps of improvements of 100 at a time. If you want to run a marathon or fun run and you haven't run for years, chunk it down to realistic yet challenging not self-defeating proportions; one mile, two miles, etc. or even half a mile, three-quarters of a mile or one mile, etc. A person with a new skill takes time to adjust in the same way as a person with a new heart transplant. In reading biographies of successful people it's apparent that they shared common ground in dreaming of doing what they did do, but they focused on each step in turn first.

Date Expected

The date expected is important as you must have lots of little deadlines. A goal without a deadline is a delusion. A deadline is to goal-setting what a trigger is to a gun – it is the essential activating mechanism. It alerts your body chemistry, creates a challenge within you to which you respond mentally and helps you maintain the all-important positive attitude.

Date Achieved

I have put the date achieved in to remind you that deadlines must be handled with mature understanding. They are, as I have said, the slave not the master. You can set them and change them. I have found that individuals are influenced by the expediency factor on setting a deadline. They want it as soon as they possibly can, which is understandable, and set the earliest possible date. If they don't achieve 'the' date based on their inexperienced calculations due to unforeseen circumstances, they feel they have failed their goal completely. This is of course nonsense as a deadline can be re-adjusted and re-set similar to a plane's expected time of arrival having to change after encountering bad weather.

By recording the date achieved you can monitor your progress in case you have to readjust your overall target date. As you approach the last of your stepping action steps and its mini-deadlines, you will be able to confidently gauge your overall target date. You will feel yourself grow in confidence as you record all these mini-successes.

Results: Fair, Good, Excellent

To monitor your performance on each step there is a section for results: fair, good, and excellent. Simply put the mark in the box. Your honesty will guide you, and as well as providing praise for a positive result it will provide an intangible message of 'come on you know you can do better' if required. After all, if you are the recorder be firm with yourself and not harsh – it is still a positive result – remember these stepping stones are a progress report, the end result is what you want, which will come to you because of lots of little successes.

Price in Hours

In the box 'price in hours', simply mark the time spent on your goal each day. This almost acts as a guide for you to be consistent in approach to what you have to do to attain your goal. It also shows you the price in time you are paying. As the word 'time', which is your most valuable resource, can be substituted for the word 'life', it will make you appreciate your efforts towards your goal.

Reward Received

Where there is 'reward received' make certain you give yourself a reward and tick the box. Too many goals have been lost purely because of the lack of a built-in reward praise system. Individuals go for weeks, months, years with no 'pat on the back' and then give up their dream when their motivation is at a low. The reasons why and the major benefit will take them over obstacles but there need to be lots of little personal 'well dones' to lubricate the journey.

So many people run their homes and businesses on the basis of communicating to their children, spouses, employees, subordinates, friends and colleagues when they have done something wrong, or forgotten to attend to something. My experience with management is that they tend to find fault and any form of praise is looked upon as a weakness. Yet we all know that a short statement of praise makes us double our efforts for the person who gave it, with a renewed vigour. Why? – so we can get some more. Millions of people go to sleep every night starving from hunger and countless millions go to sleep every night starving from praise.

Our craving for meaning and purpose is very strong. Whenever you receive praise or reward you feel appreciated, important and meaningful. So give yourself little rewards and lots of praise, no matter how small. Use the reward contract sheet that I have included. A big reward can be just telling yourself 'well done, I'm really proud of you!'

9. Overall Target Date

If your goal is, for example, reaching a certain position in your career, you will have to really think about the necessary skills you will need to acquire to reach that certain position. You will be able to get a good idea of how long it will take you to acquire those skills. The problem is not usually the time required but isolating what skills need to be required. Always remember that the target date is essential in its ability to motivate you into action but if you have to alter it do not abandon your goal. Use the date to focus on, to drive you and to aim for. You must have a date but be prepared to re-evaluate.

10. Affirmations

An affirmation in this instance is positive self-talk. We have all lived by affirmations or self-commands all our lives. Incredible though it is, we often at times live by negative ones such as: 'I am no good at making coffee, I can't speak in public, I have an awful memory, I don't like crowds', and so on. Our conscious mind is the gardener and our subconscious mind is the garden and whatever we plant in it will grow for us. Thoughts repeatedly sown will be reaped in a physical manifestation.

If you understand this you will realize that we have been programming our minds to think the way we do and consequently act the way we act for years. For each goal you must write an affirmation which puts into a statement what you will program into yourself. In fact it is sometimes wise to write several affirmations for each goal.

If, for example, you want to be more tolerant with people you will affirm to yourself: 'I am always tolerant' or 'I am becoming more tolerant every day'. Affirmations are always stated in the positive and always in the present tense. If you want to lose 20 pounds, to weigh 175 pounds you say: 'I weigh 175 pounds' not 'I must lose 20 pounds' or 'I will lose 20 pounds' or 'I am too heavy' or 'I am overweight'.

Now your subconscious will initially react with a reply such as: 'Don't be ridiculous' or 'don't kid yourself'. Why? Because it is acting in a manner consistent with your original programming. When we practice affirmations, the laws of reinforcement begin to work. People who repeatedly say to themselves and others: 'I am just not any good at making a speech' are practicing a negative kind of affirmation. What they affirm inevitably comes to pass. They think failure, affirm it and at every appropriate occasion experience a self-fulfilling prophecy.

REWARD CONTRACT CHART
Effective date   to
When   then
When   then
When   then
When   then
When   then
When   then
Weekly Bonus
Period Bonus
I PROMISE TO REWARD MYSELF *ONLY* WHEN I HAVE EARNED IT. **Date ....   Signed ....**

REWARD CONTRACT CHART

Effective date 4 May   **to** 29 June

When I make three calls each day   **then** I will enjoy a glass of wine

When I book an appointment each day   **then** I will read my magazine

When I complete my letters each day   **then** I will have my favorite dinner this week

When I study French one hour each day **then** I will go fishing this week

When I exercise ten mins every day   **then** I will watch my favorite television program

When I finish my 'to do' list every day **then** I will enjoy a video of my choice on Friday night

Weekly Bonus
When I achieve my goal for each and every day and for everything listed then I will take my spouse out for dinner or a show

Period Bonus
When I achieve my goal for each period stated above then I will celebrate by going on a week-end trip with my family

I PROMISE TO REWARD MYSELF *ONLY* WHEN I HAVE EARNED IT.

Date ..... 4 May ..... **Signed** ..... I.M. Somebody .....

So, if you state your new positive affirmations just once, you will unconsciously reject it, because we are all conditioned to judge the future almost solely on what has happened in the past. You know what your past performance has been and if you are a chronic procrastinator, for example, you will unconsciously reject any affirmation that has to do with action. The massive resistance you experience, however, will get weaker and weaker until the situation is reversed, and you unconsciously act in a manner consistent with your new affirmation. For that reason you must continually state your affirmations.

Affirmations are admittedly hard to accept at first but you only have to repeatedly use them to see that they really work. To increase their intensity you should say them out loud, with emotion, as often as possible. In this way they are driven deep within you until they become internalized and your manner and bearing act accordingly. If you want to increase your self-esteem, your affirmation would be: 'I *like* myself!' If your goal is to earn more money, say $100,000 per year, your affirmation would be: 'I earn $100,000 per year'. If you want more energy and well-being your affirmation would be: 'I feel fantastic' or 'I feel terrific'. In the past you may have used: 'Not bad, not too bad' or 'Just my luck' or 'That always happens to me'. From now on be aware of what you are saying as everything counts. Affirmations become the truth of what we believe and live by. They form a template on which we can trace out the life we want to lead.

All affirmations must be stated in the present tense and positively as I have exemplified. Where, however, you are affirming a tangible object such as a new car or house, you would not say: 'I own a such and such car or house, etc.', you would say: 'I earn an income capable of buying a such and such car or house, etc'.

All our goals must be mentally accomplished before they can become materially accomplished. As we are bound by the self-imposed limited expectations of our subconscious we must use affirmations to free our untapped potential in order to achieve everything we want. Remember the person who says 'I can' and the person who says 'I can't' are always both right.

To give you a guide on how to fill in your goal sheet I have provided you with one using weight as an example. Keep it simple but with as much relevant information, in particular reasons as to why you want to achieve the goal and how. Always use the other side of your plan sheet for additional notes.

Take a look at the completed example of the reward contract. This is an all-important agreement with yourself to bring about the necessary changes on a regular basis to attain your goal.

The contract is self-explanatory and although the example is devoted to various improvements and selling objectives you can use it for anything from losing weight to learning new skills. It doesn't matter how small or ridiculous the rewards may initially appear, as long as they mean something to you, this system works.

You will see that the 'whens' are on a daily basis whereas the bonuses are on a weekly basis. This can be adapted if you wish. Be flexible to suit yourself but try and make the reward fit the action. If for some reason you are unable to carry out a certain task on a particular day due to some unforeseen circumstances, don't become despondent. Be mature and reassess the situation and reward accordingly. The importance of this exercise will be highlighted when you start to respond with new behaviors, habits and attitudes.

Imagine someone promised you, for example, a $100,000 per year job in 18 months' time. You were also told that you had to make certain sacrifices. What would you do? – you would just get on and do whatever was necessary. Why? – because the promise was guaranteed. It is because we can't usually see the promise that we begin to wonder if we will ever succeed. Remember a 1,000-mile journey starts with taking the first step. Whenever you hear of a success story be assured that there have been many little steps along the way. Your reward system, while building up all your vital new habits, makes it all worth it. How do we keep going when we don't see the end result? Easy. We make certain we can see it. We ...

Rehearse with Imagination

Knowing that they have to first achieve mentally what they want to accomplish materially, successful people from all walks of life rehearse in their mind's eye first. They literally practice in their imagination. They see the end result. Over 13 million in Britain watched enthralled as Linford Christie proved he was the fastest man in the world when he won the 100-metre Olympic gold in Barcelona in 1992. He said:

> *The Olympics is the pinnacle of every athlete's career. They said I was too old but I did it. I had practised in my mind and saw myself do it.*

Television pictures of him in the last few moments before the race showed a man who was totally oblivious to what was going on around him – his steely concentration was so intense, it was said at the time he was 'stoned on adrenalin'.

Nothing was going to distract him. In his mind he had won the race even before he had started. The prospect of defeat was unthinkable. His determination was unshakeable.

Frank Dick, the British National Director of coaching, had stressed the importance of mental power saying that the quality that separates winners from losers: '... is what goes on behind the eyes'. Dr Barry Cripps, the British Olympic team sports psychologist, said: 'his eyes were fixed staring towards the end of the track ... he knew he was going to win'. Linford was in control of the situation, having programmed his mind to 'visualize' a successful outcome.

Unfortunately, many people are not using their imagination positively, creatively, enslaved by allowing their imagination to run away out of control, inevitably suffering from self-images of failure leading to non-goal attainment.

It's actually simple to take control of your own imagination because the brain and the nervous system cannot tell the difference between what is real and what is vividly imagined. Imagine the outcome you want and not what you don't want. Your brain tells you what to do in the future based on its knowledge in the past. The only way you can see the future is through your imagination.

Too often, however, people don't exercise the control they have and they allow their imaginations to destroy their potential by picturing situations of the past, in which they have failed. Most do not use the art of 'visualization' to their best advantage. Instead of bringing the past into the present you must practice bringing the future into the present.

To illustrate what I mean, think of a car. Your mind will see a car very quickly but like most people it will be hazy. If I ask you to start describing the car you will re-focus, because I am giving you more precise instructions. You will probably describe your own car. That's the way most of us respond in life. Our minds get by on the minimum of effort. If you want a particular car as a goal, for example, you must see the type of car you want down to the last detail. At the first occasion go into a showroom, sit in the car of your dreams and go for a test drive. Get a picture of it. Get a picture of you sitting in it. All this helps to ignite your imagination.

Sports' psychologists use visualization methods all the time to give their clients the winning edge. Why? Because the visualized thought data is fed into the brain and the entire bodies' chemistry receives the message clearly. The muscles and all actions respond appropriately to the precise instructions the visualization has commanded.

If you take a picture with your camera and are 10 per cent out of focus then the resulting photograph will be 10 per cent out of focus. If you use 10 per cent 'out of focus' with regard to the visualization of the goal you want to attain, then your goal will be distorted accordingly.

I have a business colleague who visualized the house she was working towards in her mind's eye. She visualized everything from the style, the architecture, the interior, right down to the front door. She later found the house she was looking for right on schedule.

On the other side of the coin many people have built their dream homes only to be disappointed as there were so many items they overlooked – they never vividly imagined what they wanted and consequently received an 'out of focus' result.

See Yourself

When improving yourself you must 'see' yourself as already having the traits and qualities you want to acquire. The thought always comes before the action. Before we can be, we must become, and before we can become we must be able to visualize what we want, our goals and our results.

Practice the following exercise: imagine yourself in a cinema. Make it a comfortable, relaxing place. What do you notice around you? Pay attention to detail. What colors are the walls, ceiling, seats, and curtains? The curtain opens and the screen lights up with a picture of someone you really like. Make the picture bigger and closer to you. Notice any changes in your feelings. Make the picture smaller and further away. Make it disappear in the distance and re-appear. Again notice how your feelings change. Make the picture out of focus more and more, then bring it back into sharp focus. Turn it into black and white. And then in rich color. Experiment and notice your feelings. The more clear and vivid and colorful your image the more strong your feelings. The weaker, smaller and further away the image the weaker your feelings.

Visualization is crucial to your success and one of the main reasons we have an imagination. It is not there to make us afraid all the time, to be filled with worries, doubts and fears. It is to get a jump on the future, to assist us in becoming what we are intended to become and use our potential. Use it, don't abuse it.

Neuro-linguistic Programming

There is a science known as NLP – Neuro-linguistic Programming, first developed by scientists John Grinder and Richard Bandler. It is a very powerful methodology using visualization. Anthony Robbins, one of its main exponents, teachers and walking success stories, has literally helped thousands of people reach peak performance as well as changing life-long phobias. In his book, *Awaken the Giant Within*, he states:

> *all of our feelings are based on the images we focus on in our minds and the sounds and sensations we link to those specific images. As we change the images and sounds, we change how we feel.*

Visualize, imagine, concentrate on what you want, see it! See it vividly and your feelings will respond in a positive way, your physiology will respond to your commands. Any difficult situation, no matter what, speaking in public, or going for an interview, rehearse it in your imagination first. You have your own practice arena all the time so make use of it. Climb into your movie screen at any time and see yourself having already achieved what you want.

30-Day Mental Diet

In the same way that a house is built one step at a time your progress will be made one step at a time. The step-by-step principle is the only intelligent way to attain any formidable yet worthwhile goal. It is the way you learned how to drive, it is the way all the great discoveries have been made, all inventions have been created and all abilities and talents have been perfected.

It is important to start moving towards your goal by making the next task you do a step in the right direction. At every step ask yourself the question: 'Is this leading me to where I want to go?' If not, change course, if yes, continue forward. We do not make one big jump to success so an excellent plan is to set 30-day time periods for accomplishment. This will build the habit of success. This self-investment in yourself will be the most profitable you will ever make.

Whether you have been introduced to goals before or not, it is important to get into a routine of spending time on their planning. This takes time, so for a 30-day period starting from now, you must change certain of your routine behaviors to allow you the time you require.

Work out how much time you spend reading the news-paper, listening to the news, watching the adverts on television, watching violent programs per night. Every day we expose ourselves to a diet of horror, pain, gloom and doom and torture. The average person witnesses three murders a night in the comfort of his or her own home while watching television. That's 1,000 deaths per year. Everything counts. Do you think that will have an effect on your thinking and attitude? Of course it will.

Martyn Lewis, the BBC newsreader, launched an inter-national campaign to change media values. He claimed that television news 'is a distorted mirror of events', that good stories are dropped in favor of harder news. No wonder, when greeted the average response is 'not too bad'. What happened to 'I feel great, how are you?' He launched his campaign amidst news of IRA bombing in London, a bus strike, a mini-cab driver fighting for his life after being shot, and a mother of a four-year-old fire victim charged with murder, atrocities in Bosnia, a plane crash in India and whether hard-line anti-terrorists tactics should be adopted in Britain. The only up-beat item was about the House of Lords' case about thousands of people being under threat of losing their homes after acting as guarantors for failed businesses. Even the weather forecast was gloomy! If you have a daily diet of that do you think it's going to affect your attitude? Of course it is! If you drank too much one night you'd feel in a bad way the following day. If you kept at it you would get more used to it until you were not too conscious of the effect of drink. Your body would adapt accordingly, until it wouldn't adapt any more. Everything counts.

For this 30-day diet cut your time in reading the paper to a few minutes or cut them out completely for 30 days. You'll feel the change. Your increased awareness will pick up the items that interest you. Invest the time you are saving in your planning time. You must put down in writing all your goals and plans. You haven't a moment to lose. Get right down to it. Cut TV down just to the programs that will take you to where you want to go. If there is a particular film you want to see, schedule it into your reward system.

To kick-start your 30-day diet live the first 48 hours as if they were your last days on earth, while still going about your business. Would you live it to the full or spend all the time moping and moaning? Be nice to people, feel good, smile. Who cares if people think you're crazy. It's good to feel crazy, non-conforming, alive and living your life.

Okay; for the next 28 days get up 30 minutes earlier. Get your goal book and start putting your ambitions in the organized format as shown. Work on your plans, see yourself being the person you want to be, doing and having the things you want to do and have. The time will fly by, but stop as soon as 30 minutes are up. You may want to continue but don't. Start the rest of your day on a high.

Say to yourself and others who greet you that you feel fantastic (if you genuinely don't and obviously don't want to lie say: 'I feel unbelievable!'). On any occasion when you would normally take a break from what you are doing and read something, then read something of interest that will take you where you are going. Something motivational, something which will stir your imagination or creativity.

When you drive to work don't listen to the radio, listen to an audio-learning tape – something that will take you where you want to go. Something that will improve an area or skill that will help you to attain your goal. Amazingly enough the amount of time the average person listens to the car radio during the course of one year is equivalent to over one whole university term! One of the best ways to learn is to listen to audio-cassettes.

How much of a difference do you think it would make in your life if you spent the equivalent of 20, 40-hour weeks studying instead of listening to the car radio?

Avoid Moaners

During your day be with the right people. Avoid moaners and gossipers. Leaders don't moan. They rise to the challenge. One leader's reaction to moaners when I asked him was: 'If they're not part of the solution then they are part of the problem and a problem is never solved by moaning about it'.

Your choice of peer group will be a key determinant to success or failure in your life. A conversation will act like affirmations to you as they feed you with their own positive or negative views. If there is no one to talk to, then read. Continue to feed your mind with what you want. Some people won't like what you are doing. Why? Because as you grow it may start to reflect their inadequacies. Some will even get quite aggressive. Do you know that 'men of the road' have been disposed of by their 'colleagues' for not being or becoming one of them, not being an alcoholic or even worse trying to claw back up the ladder of self-respect again.

Every evening cut down on your TV time in order to bring up the quota that you have read during one day to one hour. Only one hour a day will mean one to two books a month, which means 12 to 24 books a year in a world where the majority of people never finish one book after leaving school. Spread your reading material. Read your professional or trade journal, read self-help material and read some fiction that you enjoy.

Review your goals every morning and make sure you take some action however small towards their attainment. At the end of 30 days you will have a much clearer idea of what you stand for, what you believe in, what your values are and what is important to you. You will have defined your goals, which will have changed in the 30-day period as you begin to understand yourself more and what you really want. You will feel increased confidence and self-esteem and you will begin to feel that your life has meaning and purpose, that you count for something, that you are not just anybody, that you are somebody.

> The winds of grace blow all the time
> All we need to do is set our sails
>   *Ramakrishna*
>
> *and*
>
> What we vividly imagine, ardently desire, enthusiastically act upon, must inevitably come to pass.
>   *Colin P. Sisson*
>
> *So*
>
> Ask, and it will be given you.
> seek, and you will find;
> Knock, and it will be opened to you
>   *Luke* 11.9

THOUGHTS FOR SOWING

1. Your desire to be, do and have is the most powerful medicine in the world.

2. All great achievements are the result of a series of many small achievements.

3. There is moving forward or falling back – the world does

not stand still for any individual. Everything counts: there is no neutral.

4. The more you share the more you have. Share what is good in you and watch it multiply, withhold what is bad and watch it diminish.

5. I feel happy! I feel healthy! I feel terrific!

Chapter 5

Understanding the Evolving You

Applying Principles of Self-improvement

A colleague closed an informative talk with: 'the trouble with things being said and done, there is too much said and not enough done'. We can all appreciate that saying we will do something is inevitably easier than actually doing it.

As you start applying principles of self-improvement you will inevitably begin to evolve in a direction that is beneficial and harmonious to you. You may start noticing almost imperceptible changes in your attitude and behavior or major ones, but you will feel at some time a 'natural' resistance to the changes you are experiencing. Certainly your family and close friends will. As a result of your former internalized conditioning your subconscious is merely acting in a way that it is familiar with. It makes no difference that the changes are for the better, it is simply acting in accordance with dominant entrenched instructions. In the absence of new instructions being constantly repeated and internalized, it will continue to give 'new ways a try' and then revert back to its consistent path.

In carrying out a mental diet for 30 days it is easy to start with all the necessary motivation, but after a week or more, our dutiful subconscious gets us back on our 'old' track. The important thing to remember is to keep your thoughts on your objectives and not the things you desire to change. In addition to this, remember to think of the actual step you are taking at any one time. For example, with a 30-day mental diet think of only one day at a time and then repeat it. That is exactly the way you build up a habit initially.

Some people have difficulty in benefiting from self-help books because they follow through with an attitude of wishing, not knowing. It is a quite understandable attitude. For example, you may be living in very humble circumstances and may aspire to a better home, different furniture, another car and money in the bank, etc. When asked to follow the instructions of many self-help books you are asked to imagine yourself as already enjoying everything that you are striving for, instead of viewing the conditions which exist. As the picture of reality is so vivid in your mind it can often neutralize the picture you are attempting to establish.

As the brain and the nervous system cannot differentiate between what is real and vividly imagined it is important that the picture of what you want becomes the dominant one. If not the old enemy of self-doubt gets a strong foothold and can start switching off your self-motivation as your lack of belief grows. The good news is that as you start inevitably pulling away from your self-limiting beliefs you become stronger in self-confidence and start being aware, or conscious of the positive improvement evolving within you.

'Conditioning Statements'

To facilitate this it is a very good idea to record your goals and affirmations onto an audio-cassette tape. Record your goals and ambitions generally and record in the second person: for example: 'you are becoming more confident every day'. You are tolerant and patient with others. You always listen and let people finish. You understand others. Your improved qualities and traits are noticed and liked by others. You are respected. You are becoming more highly thought of. You always make decisions when required and with confidence. You are moving towards the top of your chosen career. You enjoy health and lots of energy. You eat healthily and enjoy your regular exercise routine. Your family and friends love you as you are always kind, considerate and thoughtful. You are kind, not weak. You are humble, not timid. You are bold, not a bully. You are thoughtful, but not lazy. You are popular. You are yourself. You have the courage of your convictions. You keep your own counsel. You are yourself. You enjoy happiness and freedom in what you want to do.

Record also the house that you see yourself living in, the car you see yourself driving, the courses you want to take, the holidays you will enjoy, the relationships you want to start or improve. Use short sentences but vivid language to spark your imagination. This will come with practice but the important thing is to see what you want in 'focus'.

After generally talking about your goals and how you see yourself move onto your affirmations about your goals. Each affirmation should be repeated five times and said with feeling, for example, 'you *like* yourself'. 'You *really* like yourself'. Each time you record leave a pause so that you will have time to repeat when you are listening to it: 'I like myself. I *really* like myself'. Other examples could be: 'You *feel* terrific, you really do'. 'You have an *excellent* memory and enjoy *excellent* concentration'. 'You are *completely* successful at everything you do'. 'You are a *total* winner'. 'You enjoy *excellent* health and energy'. 'You run your *own* company'. 'You *weigh* 175 pounds, you look *terrific*'.

An alternative is to simply use 3 × 5 cards to act as your affirmation reinforcers, and at every opportunity read them until they are internalized. Many individuals have enjoyed significant results just from the cards, which are simple, easy to use and can be regularly renewed and updated.

Please use some method of reinforcement. With all the hustle and bustle of life and its situations it is easier if you put aside 'your time'. **Remember, for things to change you have to change**.

Conscious, Subconscious, Unconscious

The use of this method is based on the fact that your subconscious mind or creative mind never sleeps and is always susceptible to suggestions. To explain very briefly the differences between your conscious mind, your subconscious mind and your unconscious mind let me use the following example: I look at the clock. My conscious mind registers that it is 5.00 pm. My subconscious mind tells me that I have an appointment with someone at 5.30 p.m. Years later when I have forgotten the time, place and whom I had to meet, my unconscious mind will have it stored. The unconscious mind is that level of mind the activity of which we are not aware during our everyday life. We know it is there because much of our behavior is controlled by it. Our irrational fears, phobias and complexes are harbored there, with its secrets only being made known to us through psychology and hypnosis. When we internalize something by constant affirmation and repetition our subconscious mind causes us to act in a manner accordingly.

The unconscious mind regulates all functions of the body. It has many other functions too numerous to mention here, but understand that as it registers everything you do – we can again see the importance of why 'everything counts'.

Unusual Yet Aware

Watch yourself becoming more aware of what you are doing and how you are evolving as you go through the 30-day period. If for some reason you stop or fall off, start again. Keep at it until you will find your awareness will have changed to the point that you will start to become conscious of those actions which are inconsistent with your beliefs, values and goals. What happens? Well as soon as you recognize that you are 'slipping back' you make a conscious effort to stick to the course you know is good for you. You will eventually find it so easy that you no longer have to work so hard at it. It has started to become your second nature. As a result of the way you are evolving, your understanding will accept the different and positive opportunities and events that will start presenting themselves to you.

Remember the reasons why so few people ever reach the top is because the large majority of people are negative thinkers. The principles you are learning in this book will raise you to undreamed of heights. To ensure that you remain there you must continue to replace negative thoughts with positive ones – it could be quite easy to go back to where you were. That is why it is important to reach the point where offsetting negative thoughts with positive ones becomes second nature. The extent of your success depends entirely upon your state of consciousness.

Every day make sure you never allow a negative thought to remain in your mind. As your conscious mind can hold only one thought at a time, eliminate a negative thought by doing something positive.

Every night decide on what you are going to achieve the following day and go to sleep with positive happy thoughts. If when you have turned the light off there is something still gnawing away at you, get up and write whatever it is down, finishing with the statement: 'I will take action to resolve this tomorrow'. You will often find you will have the answer when you wake up, but at least you will have taken some positive action by crystallizing your thinking.

Every morning start your day with enthusiastic anticipation and expectation. Let your first words start your day with enthusiasm: 'It's going to be a great day today'. Others may think you are not normal and they will be right. Why? Because the word normal is misused for usual and it is 'usual' for people to wake up and say: 'Oh dear, it's raining again, I expect the traffic will be chaotic as normal'. Only a few 'unusual' people of every generation claim their birthright of a successful life by their positive outlook, their belief in themselves and their abilities, and their action towards it; whereas the majority of usual people 'go to their graves with their music still in them' as Oliver Wendell Holmes said.

Tell yourself that the day people stop talking about you is the day you stop growing and become 'normal'. There are many statues raised to great individuals who have been criticized, but not one has been raised to a critic. Doers do. Critics blame and complain.

Test and Invest

As you begin to build up experience in setting daily, weekly and monthly goals you will begin setting more long-term goals and life-time plans. Finding true purpose will be discussed later but for the moment how will you know if your goals are 'right' for you?

There is nothing more frustrating than spending enormous amounts of time and energy to achieve goals that just don't satisfy. When you have written out each goal you must 'test' it by asking yourself questions. You have to ask yourself: 'Is this goal really what I want?' See yourself having the goal. Do you like it, are there certain problems that make it not so desirable? For example, having a beautiful boat might be a lot of fun, but the trouble in maintaining it may outweigh the pleasure in owning it. It may be that the maintaining part is part of your wanting it or it may be that you prefer to have the money to charter one whenever you want.

Is the goal possible? Be realistic here. Running a marathon is probably possible for you, but being in the Olympics may not be. Is this goal worthy? Does the goal hurt anyone? Does it violate what you think is right and proper for yourself and others? Are you willing to pay the price to reach the goal? Be realistic about the work you will have to do and the necessary sacrifice you will have to make to reach it. Is it really worth it to you?

By asking these types of questions you can eliminate wasted time and energy and avoid frustration and disappointment. I am not talking about the type of questions which refer to whether you can obtain the goal. These I have already discussed, but remember the 'rationale' will always throw up good reasons why you shouldn't undertake things. The questions I mean to ask in reality are a test of desire and self-confidence. If your answer is 'no' then what you are saying is that you don't have the necessary desire to attain the particular goal. It won't be worth the price you will have to pay and part of that price is determination which comes from desire. If the answer is 'no' then reject the goal but do so knowing why you do so. This is important as you don't want to risk any hidden guilt haunting you later as to why you didn't go after that particular goal.

When you answer 'yes' your desire and determination are massively intensified. It means the goal is firmly aligned with your system of values. At this point you will automatically begin to build the necessary dedication, determination and belief to make your plan succeed in spite of what people might say, think or do.

Your day has 1440 minutes in it. Each day invest just 1 per cent of that time in a study, thinking and planning session and you will be amazed at what rewards those 14 minutes will do for you. As you have decided your goal is important to you, take action each day towards its attainment. Don't be like the old gentleman I knew who would regularly get his plans out and study them, and then carefully put them away and never even make a start – he was waiting for the right moment to start. Whatever your goal is, when you know it is worth it to you, study and prepare yourself so that when an opportunity presents itself you will instantly recognize it and be prepared to do what is necessary.

Ten Attainment Actions

To assist you in getting started towards your journey of self-improvement I have compiled ten qualities which when developed and while being developed project you on your path to whatever it is you want to attain. Under each quality to attain I have listed several principles aligned to them.

1. Build Confidence

(a) Realize that your principal goal in life is to be happy and confidence is a state of happiness. Practice being happy and begin with smiling.

(b) Use your imagination to enthusiastically visualize that you are a positive person.

(c) Each time you initiate action always remember your past successful experiences. When you evoke these feelings, you will feel successful and act with confidence. Each time say: 'I am confident' and this in turn will evoke feelings of confidence instantly.

(d) Accept all your negative feelings as a challenge. Confidence is merely the ability to rise above negative feelings, failure and mistakes.

(e) Believe in yourself actively not passively. Confidence comes from belief.

2. Overcome Frustration

(a) Begin everything with enthusiasm. Always stop when you are enjoying what you are doing just before it becomes frustration. Return to it with renewed enthusiasm as you will look forward to it because you left it as a positive point.

(b) Become involved in a new goal. By thinking of a new worthwhile goal you can reach, your frustration will disappear.

(c) Concentrate on one thought at a time, one action at a time, one goal at a time: the more you concentrate, the less time you will have for frustration. Edison, perhaps the greatest inventor who has ever lived, and who patented over 1,000 commercial items including the light bulb and phonograph, would concentrate solely on what he was doing at that particular time and not do lots of other things at the same time.

3. Develop Compassion, Forgiveness and Understanding

(a) Forgive yourself and others. Don't be judgemental.

(b) Be agreeable with others. Don't argue, try to understand.

(c) Compliment others. Be interested in them. Express don't impress. Express builds a bridge, impress builds a gulf.

(d) Make others feel important. Don't engage in constructive criticism.

(e) Love your neighbor as yourself. Always remember that the majority of what you will accomplish will be as a direct result of how you get on with other people.

4. Develop Communication and Rapport Skills

(a) Seek first to understand before you make yourself understood. Your experiences may not be appropriate for their problem. Try to understand their situation before you advise. Remember the propensity to give advice is as great as the propensity to ignore it.

(b) Your listeners won't care what you say until they know that you care.

(c) Practice internal enthusiastic self-praise continually. Understand that how you think and feel determines how you communicate with others.

(d) Always remember that the way you perceive and see your world is not through the same lens that other people will view their world.

5. Develop a Major Absorbing Obsession

(a) Anything in life worth having is worth working for. It's not the amount that counts, it's the philosophy of your plan. If you are totally absorbed with what you really want to achieve the world will make a path for you.

(b) Always seek to learn from your adversity as this is often the doorway to where you want to go. How else can Nature direct you to the path for you? It is one way that she can make you pay attention.

6. Develop Persistence

(a) The more you can persist in the face of all your obstacles the more the belief and confidence in you grows.

(b) Only through persistence will you become what you want. Affirm to yourself: 'there is always a way – my persistence will find it'.

(c) Take Winston Churchill's success motto for your own: 'Never give up, never, never give up'. The difference between the ordinary and the extraordinary is that little bit extra. Always keep going.

7. Develop an Expectant Winning Attitude

(a) Do not 'expect the worst and hope for the best'. What an absolutely ridiculous statement to affirm. Our expectations almost always become our reality. Always affirm: I expect the best and get it.

(b) Always look to create a win–win situation with others. Don't accept that if one wins another one has to lose. With an attitude of positive expectancy you will find that you and all around you enjoy winning results. Project yourself as a winner who creates other winners too.

(c) Project a positive self-image of you being an enthusiastic person. Enthusiasm is incredibly contagious and will affect almost anyone it touches.

8. Accept 100 per cent Responsibility for You

(a) Always remember that you are the person responsible for how you feel. It's not the circumstances or conditions that is the problem, it's how you react to the circumstances or conditions of the problem that's the real problem.

(b) Don't look to blame someone or something for whatever has happened or happening, look to find the solution. There are some individuals who spend more time ensuring there is someone to blame in case what they undertake goes wrong than spending time doing what they actually undertake. Blame looks backward while responsibility looks forward.

(c) Your self-responsibility will become stronger in direct relation to eliminating your negative feelings and emotions. Each time one of your negative emotions rises up discard it by saying: 'I am responsible for the way I feel.'

(d) Immediately you stop making excuses you will be on the way to the top as you have taken complete responsibility for yourself.

9. Develop the Courage to Do What It Takes

(a) Responsibility and courage go hand in hand. Whatever you fear address the situation that causes it. Aristotle said:

> *Fear is pain arising from anticipation.*

So seldom do we do the thing we fear that we never discover if our anticipation was accurate. Fear breeds lack of experience, lack of experience breeds ignorance, and ignorance breeds more fear. It is a vicious circle summed up so well in the acronym: False Evidence Appearing Real.

I remember walking along the Copacobana in Rio de Janeiro when out of the corner of my eye I saw a snake moving furiously towards me. I jumped the highest jump I had ever jumped and kept jumping until I realized it was a rubber snake on a piece of wire. Now my inbuilt alarm system had gone off appropriately causing the adrenalin to fuel my jump. That false evidence, however, spawned the beginning of a real fear of snakes. Having experienced this FEAR on various occasions I decided to address it. I read a book on snakes and even went to a place where I could handle them. My fear of them vanished. I understand them, I understand to take care where snakes could be, but I am no longer scared of them.

Each time in business when I needed the courage to do something, I found the best way was to do it anyway. Only by doing what it takes will you develop the courage required. It is not the other way around. Courage comes from experiencing the thing that worries you. Courage is not the lack of fear, it is the wisdom to act in spite of fear. The best way to build up courage is to encourage yourself with: 'you can do it!'. 'En' is a prefix meaning 'to be at one with'. So don't listen to people who discourage you. Always remember that courage is doing what you are afraid to do and there can be no courage unless you are scared.

(b) The willingness to do creates the courage to do. Just by simply starting to do what you have planned, will create an ability to do which will increase your confidence and courage. So, whatever it is, begin it, make a start. Be willing especially to follow your dream. My favorite training shoes I bought because when I was contemplating which ones to buy and if I would use them, the advertisement above them was: 'just do it'. There is no better advice to develop the courage to do something or make a decision.

10. Develop a Happiness State of Mind

(a) Many people believe that happiness is dependent on things and people external to themselves, yet when we look for happiness outside ourselves we make an unhappy mistake. We feel powerless to attain happiness and devote our lives to the pursuit of things that we know won't necessarily bring happiness. Happiness involves having the courage to live the life you choose for yourself. Becoming what you really want to become and doing what you really want to do is available through your freedom of choice. So choose what you want, begin it and your state of mind will be a happy state of mind.

(b) Your capacity for happiness can be increased simply by sharing it with others. Giving to others can be the most rewarding experience of your life, even if you start with giving your smile freely. Practice smiling in front of the mirror every day for at least 30 seconds. After the initial embarrassed feeling you'll feel great about yourself.

(c) Don't save up for happiness like so many do. They live under the misconception that you have to earn it. How and when? You are happiness. Happiness is like opportunity, it's always there if you look for it. Seize it in the same way. Being happy means now, making yourself laugh more often, not a chuckle or a grin but a really big belly laugh.

(d) Remember that unhappiness is the result of old patterns of thinking and feeling. With your new programming and affirmation: 'I feel happy' you will find a new impetus to make you the better you that you can be. The message that all the above gives you is plain and simple. Work harder on yourself than you do on anything else and your everything else will follow. Get your internal world how you want it and your external world will be as you want. In other words your outer world is a mirror which reflects what is going on in your inner world. This is the basis of perhaps one of the greatest universal laws. The Great Psychologist in the Bible said: 'As within, so without'. So remember, work on yourself and everything else will fall in place.

Examine and Re-evaluate Your Beliefs

It is not possible to understand others until we understand ourselves. Nor is it possible to evaluate other beliefs, although it is commonplace, until we can evaluate our own. You will now have started to contemplate many things about your world, which you have previously neglected to contemplate. The process of self-examination and contemplation is essential for our ultimate survival and growth.

Examination of our external world is never as personally painful as examination of the world within, and it is certainly because of that feeling that the majority of people steer away from it. Within each of us are various maps of how we see the world, and whenever the validity of those maps is challenged, by new ideas and different ways of thinking, we tend to ward them off, even aggressively. Anyone who doesn't agree with our preconceived ideas and beliefs is wrong.

When you start to experience a change in your ideas it is brought about not by 'will' but by other ideas, different levels of thinking. What we might term as an 'aha' experience is when we finally see something in a different way. New ideas take time to 'seep' into our understanding before we can fully perceive them as our own.

It is for this very reason that the repetition of affirmations is important as 'maps' entrenched in our subconscious refuse instantly to accept something new. The more bound your 'old' beliefs, perceptions and values, the more powerful your 'aha' experience will be. As you start to grow you must look deeply at your beliefs, examine them and see why you have them and if you should have them. Does something always happen to cause you to miss out just when you get near to what you want? Perhaps you believe you don't deserve success? Often a belief is based on a false conclusion or an assumption and whenever we see an opportunity we start to 'rationalize' our thinking in order to stay consistent with our belief. We actually deceive ourselves more easily than other people.

Let me illustrate what I mean. I know someone who wanted to go into business on his own. He sent off for many opportunities listed in various papers and got excited as he worked out what he could do. He had to make a decision but before doing so he thought it would be a good idea to make more enquiries. He arranged several interviews and after each interview he decided he needed more information. What happened was that he started to look around subconsciously for reasons why he should not go into business. He was not aware of what he was doing yet the more he rationalized, the more he confirmed his belief that he was being very prudent. Finally he was attracted to one advertisement and his enquiries satisfied him. What happened then is that he started to meet people who were already in a business and as there weren't too many he started to rationalize that if it was such a good proposition people should be clambering for it. There must be something that he has overlooked. Why aren't there many people doing it. After all, anything that will make him a fortune will be attractive to everybody else. Why are there only a few?

If, on the other hand, he had found lots of people doing it and making a success, he would then reason that it was an overcrowded business. Quite clearly rationalization will take facts and adapt them to suit the beliefs of the person concerned.

A few years ago I was running my various businesses from two offices. One was a rather humble refurbished block and the other was an elegant office block of 40,000 square feet in its own grounds – very exclusive. I remember interviewing a gentleman at the humble town offices who said to me at the time that he could not believe that a company that existed in these humble offices could pay him what I was offering. There had to be something odd, after all it stands to reason that it can't be right.

I suppose if he had been interviewed in my palatial block he would reason that I was making too much money out of what I was doing and not providing good value. After all, how else could there be palatial offices – it stands to reason.

It doesn't matter what the facts are, they will always be interpreted in a way to provide people with reasons for justifying their decisions.

The rationale will be discussed further later but for now ask yourself some questions, and think hard on these. Why do you believe you can't do something? Why do you rationalize almost to the point of not doing something? When you make a decision why do you have to justify it by making lots of other reasons? Whom are you convincing? Why do you need to? Could it be that you are mistaken about a certain belief? Have you cheated yourself because of some stupid belief?

Whether correct or incorrect our beliefs determine how we perceive events, creating in turn our attitudes and behaviors. This inevitably affects our relationships with others. I remember being accosted by a man who was disorientated and slurring his words. The action I was about to take was due to my perception of his drunken state. I was mistaken, however. He had unfortunately suffered a stroke and was requiring assistance. All my feelings changed instantaneously. More often, of course, beliefs change over a period of time, as you understand something in more depth.

Remember that both behavior and feelings spring from belief. To rout out belief, which is responsible for your feelings and behavior, ask yourself: 'why'? If there is something you continually hold back from ask: 'why'?

The knowledge you are acquiring about yourself now must be constantly examined and re-evaluated. M. Scott Peck says in his great book *The Road Less Traveled*

> *A life of wisdom must be a life of contemplation combined with action.*

I believe that no one else can question our beliefs and values as well as we can and that it is part of our necessary growth that we do so. Contemplation is thinking about something, often of an uplifting nature. When we hear a new and potentially good idea we tend to say: 'I'll have to think about that'. Contemplation is a good time to 'think about that', to consider the truth of it, to imagine the changes and improvements it might make in your life. Use that 1 per cent of your day, those 14 minutes if you like. The idea of contemplation, is to set aside a certain amount of time to think about just *that*, whatever you decide 'that' will be.

Keeping Life's Wheel in Balance

The lumberjacks were surprised but quite pleased that the old lumberjack had not appeared for work that day. They quite liked the old man but times were hard and if he missed the quota that he had to do, he would more than likely lose his position and they in turn would pick up his quota. They thought about the extra benefits. But they continued at the usual pace. The next day the old man was on site. During the day he not only cut down one but also cut down over two days' quotas. The other lumberjacks were amazed. They said to him: 'well you certainly made up for being away. Why didn't you turn up yesterday? You weren't ill were you?', 'No', the old man replied, 'I'm fine, I just decided to take time out to sharpen my axe'.

One of the hardest working men I know is my friend Derek Ross. Derek seems to have twice the amount of energy of people half his age. He told me that the key to having a successful life was to live a balanced life. He said: 'When the wheel of life is out of round the ride gets rough'. Derek is a man who is keen to learn from the adversity that life challenges us with. He works closely with his wife Vivienne and they literally work hard and play hard. They make certain they take time out to sharpen their axe.

We all need time to 'sharpen our axe'. Without balance we most assuredly will lose our cutting edge.

My reason for ensuring you establish values, know what you stand for and what is important to you, is to create balance in your life. Any goals' program that is not based on a priority of values is almost meaningless. Like many others I learned the hard way. Years ago I set goals and achieved them, but at what cost. There was certainly no balance in my life. In the space of a few years. I had the 'whole shooting match' as my consultant called it. High blood pressure, three duodenal ulcers, a hiatus hernia, loss of a child, divorce, loss of a company, to name a few. Nature has a way of telling you to slow up, to have balance in your life. Human beings are the only creatures who do not have balance in their lives unless they create it by choice. Mankind has to use this power of choice.

It is very difficult to decompartmentalize yourself. If you have major difficulties at the office you will tend to take them home with you and if your home life is turbulent you tend to take it to the office. The only way to ensure harmony and subsequent balance is to have defined goals aligned to your values in all areas of your life.

You will recall that I have listed six main areas: financial/ career, physical/health, family/social, personal/fun/adventure, mental/emotional, spiritual/ethical. You can re-name them to suit your values if you prefer, but what is crucially important is that you do not neglect any area. If one area is not so important, then as I have said before, recognize the fact, admit it, and assign that goal to whatever values you place on it, and adjust your other goals accordingly.

Time Out

Having the discipline to be in balance gives us flexibility which is required for successful living in all areas. The discipline of 'balance' can be learned and usually it involves giving up something. Children, for example, particularly enjoy the doing of something rather than the setting up of something. They want to get on with it, to enjoy it, and what better way to learn initially. My eldest son Jason and I were going to play a game which involved some wood battens. Many things could have done the job just as well but I wanted to do it properly and went to cut the pieces of wood. Jason understandably wanted to get on with the game and said: 'hurry up, dad' at which point my saw jumped and I almost cut my thumb off and spent the afternoon in hospital having stitches. I learned that you have to give up something about yourself to have balance. What do I mean? All the plan involved was to play a game, but my desire to set it up properly effectively meant the game was never played. I gave up that desire from then on in order that I could enjoy the moment of just getting on and doing things.

Years later when Jason bought a boat and invited me to help him, we got straight down to it. I remember that he was amazed that we finished everything we wanted to do in one day. In this way his enthusiasm and enjoyment was there from the start. After all he wanted to get it into the water — that's what boats do. A few weeks later he raced it.

Goals must be compatible and not be at cross-purposes with one another for there to be balance. This compatibility is possible by setting goals and objectifying values in every area. You can't have a goal to take your family on a luxury exotic holiday unless you have financial goals that will provide sufficient income to make saving the money possible.

You may have noticed that I have referred to 'time out' and not 'time off'. The idea that we need 'time off' comes from working for another to fulfill another's dreams. Now that your life is directed towards fulfilling *your* dream why would you want to take 'time off' from that?

Taking time out means nurturing yourself while doing a project. It does not mean not doing the project. Learn to take the pressure off while you do what you do. When you think of recreation, think of re-creating your attitude towards the work at hand. Obviously there will be activities which are more enjoyable than others. Learn to alternate more pleasant ones with the less enjoyable.

The old saying of 'a change is as good as a rest' is very true. The only 'leisure' time you need is when you sleep at night. Each time you begin to feel stagnant on a particular activity, do something else like learn a language, play football, read a book about a different subject. Many writers relax with a game of chess. The brain never stops and every time you give it variety it gets the body to respond. Think of a time when you have just finished work and the family or colleagues say: 'let's do whatever' and you say: 'no, you haven't got the energy'. They finally persuade you and what happens is that you have the energy! You can go back to work or home refreshed. Yes refreshed! Balance in your life is refreshing.

I remember teaching my little daughter, Shamira, to ride

her bicycle. When she had got the hang of it she said to me: 'It's easy, daddy. I love it. I can go anywhere I want to go, all I have to do is to stay in balance'. A little later she had a mishap and told me 'I lost my balance daddy, then I lost me'. 'Out of the mouths of babes', they say. So remember don't lose the new-found you – stay in balance.

> If the doors of perception were cleansed
> everything would appear as it is, infinite
> *William Blake*
>
> *and*
>
> What is within us is also without
> What is without us is also within
> *The Upanishads*
>
> *yet*
>
> the secret of life is balance, and the
> absence of balance is life's destruction.
> *Hazrat Inayat Khan*

THOUGHTS FOR SOWING

1. When you seek to understand someone, look at the world through their lens not yours.

2. Work on your inner world in order to strengthen your outer world.

3. Invest 1 per cent of each day's time in you and the other 99 per cent will benefit.

4. When the wheel of life is out of round, the ride gets rough. Use balance to get where you are going in one piece.

Part Three

Seek and Employ Your Purpose

Chapter 6

Learn to Listen to the Person Who Knows You Best . . . You

Silent Contemplation

I have said in the last chapter that it was important to take time out to contemplate. Only by silent contemplation can you learn to listen to your inner voice that will guide you in the right direction every time. That's right, I said every time. Can you imagine how successful your life would be if you could learn how to listen to the inner voice with such confidence and belief that you were always led to the right situation for you each and every day?

All the instructions and ideas of understanding and accepting yourself as a unique and special individual, of building beliefs in your abilities and understanding and recognizing that your inner world creates your outer world, now culminates in showing you how you can tap into a powerful source of wisdom and guidance purely for you to act upon.

Remember, ideas and different thinking take time to seep in. Our 'reasoning' and rationalization create our own self-limiting beliefs for why something cannot be so. Think of the old fable of a frog who had never ventured from the well in which he lived. One day a frog whose home was the sea came to the well. 'Where do you live?', said the frog in the well. Upon hearing the answer he then asked: 'What is the sea?' and 'Where is it?' 'It is a very large body of water and not far away' was the reply. 'How big is your sea?' 'Oh very big', was the reply. 'As big as this?', said the first frog pointing to a stone. 'Oh much bigger', said the second frog. 'As big as my well?' Again the reply: 'Oh much much bigger'. 'Well how much bigger then?' said the well frog. 'Why the sea in which I live would make millions of your wells'. The first frog said 'Nonsense, you are a dreamer and a falsifier, get out of my well. I want nothing to do with any such frogs as you'.

When students are ready, and they have to be ready, the teacher will appear. The true teacher is the one whose endeavor is to bring the one they teach to a true knowledge of themselves and hence of their own interior powers, that they may become their own interpreter.

We all have voices in our minds. Often they are internalized voices of our parents, teachers or others who were important when we were growing up. Some of these voices became part of our self-image. Some of our inner voices are helpful, but some are negative, demanding and overcritical. If we believe these voices they can severely limit us and rob us of our true potential and success. It is important to distinguish between the critic within, which must be silenced, and the guide within, which must be cultivated. Being able to listen and understand your inner voice, I believe, is one of the most important tools for reshaping your self-image and for taking charge of your life.

Often we hear our true inner voice guiding us but we choose to ignore it so often that after a while it becomes impossible to recognize. How often have you been involved in debates, discussion, conversation or say an argument and you are about to say something and a little voice inside says: 'don't say it' and you still say it anyway. As soon as the words have left your mouth you know you shouldn't have said them, that they have had a very damaging effect (on you, remember!) but you start rationalizing that you had a right to say what you did.

You may reason that if you hadn't said what you said the other would have thought you weak. You may reason that to be assertive you must speak your mind, yet your inner mind said not to speak it anyway. You may reason things out, but they will never turn out as you think they will. It will not come right that way at all. Ask the right inner voice to guide you and it will do so. If you will only follow the voice of intuition, it will speak ever more clearly and plainly until, with use, it will be absolute and unerring in its guidance.

Your Inner Voice

So what is this inner voice, where does it come from and how do you tap into it? I mentioned in the opening chapter how everyone has access to an 'inner genius' – that our mind is part of a greater universal mind. A mind if you like of infinite intelligence. It is the source of all our insights, our intuition, our creativity. When we act on a hunch or a sixth sense it is because we have chosen to act on the feeling we so strongly felt at the time. And if we acted immediately we were always proved correct. If we delayed before we acted, we found we were too late no matter what our action. And whenever we have chosen not to act and learned later of the benefit we have missed, we have reasoned why we would not have achieved it in the first place. Everyone can remember 'rare' times when the hunch has paid off. The reason they are 'rare' is because any ability that is not used, acted on or believed will become weaker.

If you take a boat out into the sea and fill a glass half full of the liquid you are floating in, that glass would be identical in composition to the ocean from whence it came. Although it is in a container the glassful and the ocean are one and the same. Part of your mind is a microcosm of an infinite ocean of wisdom and as such it has direct access to it.

Let us now take our glass of water and immerse in it up to three-quarters of a large handkerchief. Here we have a good symbol of the human mind – the fabric below the water representing the unconscious mind and the dry quarter representing the conscious mind. Now let us place a sugar lump on the dry part of the handkerchief. This represents a thought held in the conscious mind. What happens? It causes only a little impression on the handkerchief. The sweetness of the sugar is not absorbed by the handkerchief. This is precisely what happens when a thought is for a fleeting moment held by our conscious minds. It does not usually affect us to any great extent and if we cast that thought out of our mind it goes without having accomplished very much for us, good or bad.

Now let us depress the handkerchief until the whole of it is below the surface of the water carrying this sugar lump. See what happens now. The sugar rapidly dissolves into the water and in this state it now sweetens the water and the whole of the handkerchief as well. This is an analogy of what happens when a person falls asleep with a thought held clearly in the conscious mind. The thought is borne down into the subconscious mind where it pervades in a most effective manner, the whole mind of the sleeper. Remember this when you are trying to impress upon your mind the great future you desire to achieve.

Just as the composition of the water in the glass was the same as that in the ocean, so are your thoughts related to your mind and if you understand this fact you will be able to understand the relation between your total mind, conscious and subconscious and the infinite and universal mind.

Whatever your beliefs and whatever names you apply to your beliefs, creator, reason for creation or existence, anything that is created must be created for a cause. Even the reasoning mind agrees with that. The major part of your mind is there for a purpose, a receiving set through which all ideas and thoughts in harmony with our definite purposes and plans can be flashed, registered and sent out. When you focus on what you want, your mind will 'tune in' to the various messages that the infinite intelligence or universal mind is sending out.

What I am saying is that you have access not only to all the data stored into your subconscious mind but also access to all data *outside* your experience. To the degree that we open ourselves to this spirit of infinite wisdom it manifests itself to us and through us. In this way we can link in to the very heart of the universe. With belief and confidence in this innate ability we do not have to go to another for wisdom and knowledge. We should always look upon others and books as teachers and not masters and more importantly agencies not sources. That is why it is so important to be true to yourself, in other words true to your own soul, for it is only through your own soul that the voice of the spirit of infinite wisdom speaks to you. This is your conscience, your intuition, your internal guide. This is the voice of the higher self, the voice of the soul, the voice of your creator.

Going into the Silence

Everything that is valuable for us to know will come to us if we will but open ourselves to the voice of this universal mind. Wisdom comes by intuition and it far transcends knowledge. Knowledge of many things may be had simply with a very retentive memory. It comes by tuition. But wisdom far transcends knowledge in that knowledge is a mere incident of this deeper wisdom.

Some people are unable to divest themselves of an intellectual pride and allow prejudices, preconceived opinions and beliefs to stand in the way of true wisdom and they reason and rationalize why something is or isn't, happens or doesn't happen. More often many people fail to tap into their innate powerful source because they confer with everybody and everything else but themselves. They go to great lengths not to be alone, to be always surrounded by others yet only by 'aloneness' can you learn to tune into your inner voice.

Going into the silence, having complete stillness, is by far the best way to learn how to activate your inner guidance voice. It is possible after practice to be able to activate this voice regardless of surrounding noise, but to start you must have complete solitude. Ask yourself when was the last time you were completely alone without any artificial noise whatsoever, literally cultivated a silence and just thought, closed your eyes, without sleeping and really thought? Can you remember a time? There is chaos and confusion in our world today. This mad state of affairs, with perpetual struggle for existence makes people live at a breakneck pace, with the days and nights crowded with things to be done. Aloneness, not loneliness, is often very difficult to procure and many would feel unhappy if they had it. Some of us cannot bear silence or being alone for more than a few minutes. This attitude must be broken down at once. Amazingly enough the deep silence of a quiet place is something most of us have never known. How then can we hear our inner voice, the voice that is constantly at work for us, trying to show us where to go and to get what we want? Simple – we cannot. A quiet place is essential, and if you have not got one, then you must reorganize your world. The task is nothing less than that.

Take Time to Think

Consider the lives of great individuals who have influenced the world, and in every case you will find that each of them spent considerable periods of time alone, contemplating, meditating and listening. Every outstanding religious leader in history, Jesus, Moses, Buddha, Lao Tzu, Confucius, Mohammed, Gandhi, spent much of their time in solitude from the distractions of life. Political and state leaders whose lasting words and actions shaped the course of history, good or bad, gained insight from solitude. Sir Winston Churchill, Disraeli, Roosevelt, Lincoln, Lenin, Stalin, Marx, Mao Tsetung, all developed their innate capabilities by spending time alone. Sometimes enforced periods in prison helped create their ideologies. Without distractions they could plan their future moves.

Leading universities require professors to lecture only a few hours per week in order that they have time to think. Without exception all outstanding business people spend a good deal of time in uninterrupted thought. They may be surrounded during the day by assistants, secretaries and reports but they take the time to confer with the person who knows them best ... themselves. They use solitude to put the pieces of a problem together, to work out solutions, to plan and to do their 'listening' to the thoughts that come to them.

The greatest people from time to time avoid the company of others. They get right away, either in a room of their own and lock the door or they walk up a hill where they can sit and quietly meditate. Make yourself a study 'away from it all' even though it is only an attic or shed. Go to this 'retreat' regularly. If you cannot do this, go high up on some hill where you can sit alone. Try to dwell alone with yourself for a short time every day. Take with you that 'listening' attitude, as though you were expecting to hear.

Try to shut out all noises and thoughts of the outside world. This will get easier with practice, but you have to shut your mind to outside things. You can do this because you can control your mind. You have just to allow thoughts to come into your mind at any moment and any kind of thought.

As often as possible and preferably every day you must work with it until you can sit in the silence for at least half an hour. You must resolve to set aside some time, preferably every day, to be completely by yourself. Perhaps early in the morning or late in the evening or during lunch, it doesn't matter when so long as your mind is fresh and free from distractions.

You may say that you just don't have the time and that every hour is spoken for. By calling a halt, being still and listening your load will be eased. You will see how best to complete your work without effort. The flashes of inspiration that make people millionaires in time come from taking time to think. Often at times people are so busy earning money that they haven't got time to make money.

Listening to Hunches

It is absolutely essential that you cultivate the art of stillness – physically and mentally. In this way that part of your mind that I shall call the super-conscious and which has direct access to the universal mind can give you ideas so illuminating that success in whatever you are doing is a certainty.

You become enormously sure of yourself. Suddenly during a session, perhaps even the first, you will find that your mind clears, that you are conscious of listening. You feel an impelling urge, a sudden impulse to act, to do something, to go somewhere or to phone someone. Feel guided. You know you must act on this guidance. You have a 'hunch', an answer, and you must act on it. You see your way to change unfavorable conditions, surmount difficulties and overcome hardships. Everything seems so obvious, clear and simple, that you wonder why you didn't think of it before. You are directed. In this moment you become your own creator.

I have scheduled below in steps when and how to go into the silence, what to do, what happens, what to expect, how you receive answers, how to know they are the right ones and when to act in order that you can commence experiencing this wonderful innate ability of yours straightaway. All you need is the desire and expectation which are the bride and bridegroom in joining with this innate gift that you do possess. The answers you will receive are *always* time-dated and must be followed immediately. Just think back for a moment. How many times have you had the feeling or urge to contact someone by letter or phone – someone in authority for example – and you don't act, letting 'sleeping dogs lie', and the very next day they phone you or you receive a letter from them. You have been pre-empted, lost your advantage, given away the control and what do you say: 'I knew I should have contacted them first'. Remember always go with your feelings not with what you ought, or should. Just by doing this a few times will get you back in touch with you and what is right for you. The more we delay our intuitive feelings to act, the more we obscure them and invite other mistaken and conflicting beliefs to provide reasons for our intuition's non-accomplishment.

Most of the time we are guided by our reasoning faculties – we choose to reason things out, but we develop our sixth sense by listening to the voice of our super-conscious and by paying attention to it. That way we are right every time.

Mind Teamwork

The key is to use the reasoning part of the mind and the intuitive part as a team not one against the other. We have the ability to use them both ways so surely it makes sense to use them in harmony with each other. Both are necessary to each other as Yin and Yang, male to female, logic to emotion. The reasoning side helps us to find, clarify, determine and research exactly what we want and by bouncing it off our intuitive feelings we make a decision and take action.

Notice that I said the reasoning side bounces off the intuitive side and not the other way about. Intuitive solutions which although always correct are often absurd and by bouncing off the reasoning side they would never become a reality. To illustrate this, picture the businessman who comes home with a massive problem he must make a decision on. He has researched all the facts and read all the reports and reasoned all the whys and wherefores. During the evening he discusses it with his wife giving her a brief outline of the various situations. Whether asked or not she may come up with an answer or suggestion which is seemingly ridiculous at first but after a while becomes blindingly obvious as the right approach, the correct decision.

Now I'm not saying that you have to be married or have a partner of the opposite sex to be in touch with intuition. I use the above example as an analogy which many will relate to. The fact is, is that we each have intuitive and reasoning sides. All of us have strong reasoning sides quite simply because our conditioned heritage has developed it. What's important is that we make a constant effort to develop our intuitive side which we can do simply by using it.

When we have used all our reasoning capabilities to straighten out a problem and have still not reached a satisfactory solution, then at that point we turn it over to our intuitive side and expect an answer. To quote Ralph Waldo Trine:

> *If the time comes when we know not what course to pursue, when we know not which way to turn, the fault lies in ourselves. If the fault lies in ourselves then the correction of this unnatural condition lies also in ourselves.*

My belief is that businesses are becoming increasingly aware of the effectiveness of the intuitive and perceptive individual. It is interesting to note that women are being employed in increasing numbers because of their intuitive abilities and quite rightly so. The power-mad 1980s saw many females coming into the business arena, but almost as if they were unsure of the identity that they should portray, they became almost 'clones' of a 'reasoned establishment'. They worked hard and there were some real success stories but their powerful innate skills of intuition were almost put to one side as they were a reminder of the 'homely little woman'. Almost to prove themselves they became 'super women' in order to overcome perhaps a basic insecurity. Fortunately the 1990s saw woman develop in her own right, secure in a sense of her own identity and ability. Certainly there will continue to be a significant increase in the number of women holding key

positions due to their intuition and perceptions coupled with
their growing confidence and self-esteem.

New Ideas Keep You Moving Forward

Companies and individuals are increasingly *remembering*
that new ideas keep you moving forward – new ideas coupled
with exciting plans, plans that form the heart of a company
or individual beliefs. Often the board of a company cannot
see the wood for the trees, they are too close to a situation or
restricted by their in-house politics. They may have various
problems to surmount which new concepts and ideas may
resolve but without an 'intuitive shot in the arm' they become
battle weary with all the 'reasoning' and end up spending the
time 'fire fighting'. A major company I was called in to advise
intuitively had a board consisting of five members. After a
fairly lengthy meeting we 'threw the rule book out of the
window'. It was agreed that the seemingly insurmountable
situation facing the board would be addressed. After discussing the problem it was decided that each board member
would, in his own time, come up with a super-conscious
solution. At the next arranged meeting 72 hours later we all
put forward our ideas. Four out of five members of the board
admitted that when they first wrote down their ideas they
were embarrassed because they thought the solutions they
had come up with were somewhat 'unusual'. They, however,
liked the simplicity of them and felt confident to put them
forward. Amazingly each one of the four had come up with
the same 'irrational' idea. The more they discussed it the more
obvious it seemed and they put it into action straightaway. It
involved the acquisition of a company which at the time was
not available, yet on contacting them the company agreed to
meet. Negotiations quickly culminated in a merger solving my

clients' 'insurmountable problem' and making them a market leader in their new specialized field.

The fifth member of the board regretted his lack of any ideas but admitted that he did not really believe in this type of solution process and 'reasoned' that his time was better spent sorting the problem in the way he was trained. Needless to say, that board regularly holds 'brain storming' sessions and each individual member also engages in 'silence solutioning' regularly. The four members who had come up with the idea accepted that they had nothing to lose, that it made sense, and that they wanted to believe it.

Moreover, in conversation later it transpired that they each 'remembered' that they used to spend a lot of time contemplating while they were building the business, but as they worked and success increased they found less time to do it. Less time to *do it!* Less time to do the thing that got them where they wanted to be in the first place. Can you relate to that? Can you think of a situation in your life in which you didn't bother to do what 'was' important because it no longer 'appeared' necessary, or you no longer had the time to spare.

What you have done or what you do at present may not be your vocation but they are vehicles towards your vocation. When you finally reach the vehicle that is your vocation remember that all 'vehicles' have basic principles they work by. The principles in this book will get you where you want to be but you have to keep using them. It is so *important* to understand this. Yes, they will become a habit *in time* but good habits are *hard* to form although easy to live with whereas bad habits are *easy* to form although hard to live with. For this reason you will have to work harder at them and all the time you will feel yourself being tugged back to the security of your 'comfort zone'. Each time you take 'quiet'

time and 'time out' your old entrenched feelings of guilt and
worry will 'reason' you into doing something else even with
the approach of 'anyway you don't have to now'. That is why
having new goals, life plans and finding true purpose is so
important in one's life and I will be covering these within this
chapter.

I speak to you from personal experience knowing that
these principles work and knowing that they stop working as
soon as you stop applying them. You must always have
another goal, a purpose. You must never become 'comfortable'. The universal laws work on you whether or not you
work with them. The super-conscious functions continuously
and whenever you take the first step towards a goal it
automatically seems to resolve any problems on the way to
achieving it. This part of your mind will respond to your goal
commands with all the ideas and energies you require. That
is why you must have already defined goals which you are
committed to.

Activating Your Super-conscious

The super-conscious operates when you are concentrating all
your thoughts on a particular situation you want the answer
to or strangely enough (yet not for the super-conscious as it
works 24 hours a day) when your mind is completely busy
elsewhere and the particular situation is furthest from your
conscious mind. You may already have experienced a time
when while you were involved in something an idea came to
you relating to another thing and you have replied 'of course,
that's a good idea'.

Whatever the goal or problem you have to deal with, or
want ideas or answers to, first define and clarify it. In doing

your research get as much information as you can and try consciously to solve the problem. Then turn it over to your super-conscious mind.

What to Do

Find a place you can be undisturbed for 30–60 minutes. Sit down in preference to lying down, although be comfortable, and make certain you have pen and paper with you. Listen to your super-conscious. Listen with an attitude of confident expectation. Close your eyes and imagine you are looking at the inside of your forehead. After some time, between 15 and 30 minutes, much less with practice, your mind will suddenly go completely clear and thoughts and ideas will start coming to you. During the whole time write down everything that comes to you. Don't leave out bits here and there because it's not what you like. You will get suggestions to go somewhere, phone somebody, do something.

What to Expect and How You Receive

Your super-conscious will bring you answers and ideas at exactly the right time you require them. They are always time-dated which means you must act on them immediately. As a result of this you may or may not get the answer you require during your sitting as tomorrow's supplies are needed only when tomorrow comes. The super-conscious will have registered, however, and give you ideas often when you are busy doing something else, because the time is then right. You will in any event feel your mind suddenly go clear and ideas and suggestions will come to you. The ideas that come to you may seem quite irrelevant at first, it may be that they are the key to opening another door in your life. In this way the super-conscious can bring you the experiences you need to be successful. Do you know that almost half of all millionaires made it by doing something completely different from what they originally started doing? Something happened which made them change course no matter how much they battled. If you want to know why something is happening to you ask your super-conscious. Most people's greatest success seems to come just after their greatest failure.

Your super-conscious will send you answers in various ways – often it will be an intuitive feeling, idea or suggestion to phone somebody. These are definitely time-dated and you must contact the person without delay. If you do delay what happens, and this has happened to me and many of my clients who have said: 'I'll do it later', is that when you do eventually get in touch with the person you were instructed to they reply with: 'I wish you'd phoned me earlier'. By then, of course, it's too late and the opportunity has passed. You may be instructed to go somewhere, somewhere you would never imagine going. While there, however, you will meet with someone and the chance encounter could lead exactly where you want to go.

A client of mine phoned me excitedly to say he was enjoying enormous success with his 'sittings'. He told me that while driving a couple of days previously he had had a tremendous urge to turn into a street for no reason. He had, however, been consciously aware of practicing to be in tune with his feelings and for this reason had turned into the street. The street turned out to be a dead end and he had to drive into an office car park in order to turn round. In the process of doing so he heard through his open window: 'Hello, Michael, fancy seeing you here'. It turned out to be not only his colleague from years before but also, more importantly, it was the person that he was instructed to contact through his last 'sitting'. The only trouble was he hadn't known how to contact him because they had lost touch years before! He had been led to this 'chance encounter' and to the offices of his old colleague and now they were doing business together. What was really important was that he had followed his feelings and not disregarded them with the usual: 'I haven't time for that'. If you could build up the habit of tuning into your feelings and taking the time to listen to them it would save you time in the long run.

How Do You Tell When the Solution is Right?

Whether it is a sitting, a chance encounter, finding something in a bookshop, reading something in a paper, phoning someone, seeing someone or going somewhere, how will you know that the answer being given to you is the right one? This is the easy part and there can be no mistaking it. When the answer comes it will be completely obvious, clear and simple. It will be simultaneously accompanied by a feeling of euphoria. You will have a burst of energy and joy. You will feel excited. You will say yes! that's it. You will feel like Archimedes when he shouted 'eureka'. Although I wouldn't advise running naked in the street as he did shouting: 'I have it, I have the answer!'

Often when you reason out a decision you feel heavy of heart, resigned to it yet obviously determined to see it through. You may say: 'Right, I've made the decision, I'm not happy with it, but there it is I have to see it through'. More often than not it may be the wrong decision. If you don't feel good *after* you made the decision no matter how difficult it was to make, how do you expect your heart to be in the action to see it through? I'm not talking 'rule of thumb' here, I am saying that any decision concerning *your* goals, *your* plans and *your* life you must feel good about. A client of mine gave up his position of 15 years to do what he had always dreamed of. It was a very hard decision for him. He had a mortgage, family and all the usual bills. His sense of security made it a very difficult decision. When he made the decision to leave, however, he told me he felt: 'really happy about it'. His happy heart, light spirit and expectant attitude carried him from strength to strength. A decision of unhappy heart, heavy spirit and disenchanted attitude has no strength to carry and barely enough to survive.

You will find that you attract people, conditions and circumstances that are consistent with your goals. In fact I will use Archimedes' story as an example. Archimedes the great mathematician was a leading adviser of King Hiero. King Hiero had commissioned from a goldsmith a crown. When he received the crown he wanted to ensure that it was in fact solid gold and not a mix of silver and copper with a covering of gold. Archimedes worked hard on the problem but could not think how to prove whether it was gold. He believed, however, that there was a way, he expected to find a way and he waited for an answer. In taking a bath he filled the bath to the brim and then got in it and his bodyweight displaced water all over the floor. When this happened he had a thought – silver and copper were half as dense as solid gold and, therefore, would have different volumes. If the gold crown was put into water the volume of water displaced could be compared with that displaced by the same weight of gold. The crown was found to be silver and copper with just a touch of gold and the poor goldsmith lost his head. It was unfortunate for the goldsmith who had lied in the first instance but Archimedes put his solution down to a super-conscious solution.

The discovery of Velcro, penicillin, x-rays, Teflon, dynamite, the Dead Sea Scrolls, iodine, small-pox vaccination and quinine all owe their discovery to intuitive inspiration. The world has progressed because of super-conscious solutions, because of individuals who have taken the time to listen to their inner selves, who have taken time to sit down and wait for ideas as opposed to hustling and bustling and getting on with life by trying to find external ways to sort out things. Why not start the habit of taking time to think for yourself and really listen to yourself and expect an answer?

When to Act

The more you visit your 'retreat' the more you will like it. The less you go, the more you will loathe it. The more often you go to it the greater comfort it will become. The reason I tell you this is in order that you understand that your ability to use it and its capability to give you the answers you require will grow as it is used and believed in. In time you will recognize the suggestion it gives you as coming from that source and you will act accordingly.

You have to resolve to build the habit of doing this as often as possible, preferably every day, as all messages you will receive are for today and not for tomorrow. They come like manna in the desert day by day, with each day bringing an adequate supply for the day's needs only. Some suggestions will involve culmination over a period of time but some form of initial action is important.

Now be honest with yourself. If you genuinely feel at this stage you are unable to devote time each day for a sitting then pick regular times, even if it is only once a week, to take serious quality time to be totally alone and undisturbed. The important thing to remember is that whenever you receive a message you must act on it *immediately*. Don't rationalize and say: 'I can't do that now' or 'I can't phone him' or 'that doesn't make sense at all, why should I want to do that' or 'I'll phone tomorrow or the weekend'. Immediately means within 60 minutes. If you can't get hold of the person then drop them a line or then try them in the evening but do take some form of action. *Don't* leave it.

Intuition Versus Rationale

Our minds use both intuition and rationale for apprehension – vehicles to provide a form of understanding. Intuition is defined as immediate apprehension by the mind without reasoning. Rationale is explained as understanding by reasoned explanation. The intuition is never wrong but it acts more as a warning on where not to go. For example, if you come to a crossroads in your life it will suggest to you the way *not* to go. People nowadays have got out of the habit of using their intuitive powers and tend to rely more on their rationale. In this way they can reason why or why not they should do such a thing. It is *not* the role of the rational mind, however, to create or to do the job at hand. Its job is to select the goals, gather information, conclude, evaluate, estimate and start the wheels in motion. It is not responsible for results.

The intuition provides through the workshop of its continual process and access to its huge universal databanks the next step to take. They are designed to work as a team. What has happened is that we use the most powerful tool at our disposal – our mind – for our disposal. Rather than dispose of barriers to our dreams, the mind disposes of the dreams.

By rationalization we spend more time inventing iron-clad, solid and impenetrable reasons why it is not even marginally possible to get something, than we spend on trying to get it. In every area of life we have one of two things: reasons or results, excuses or experiences, stories or successes. In the amount of time we give our mind to invent a watertight excuse, we could have created an alternative way of achieving the desired result.

Our 'Comfort Zone'

Why have we allowed the situation to arise when our two thought and creative processes are at odds with each other, pushing against each other instead of pulling together which is what they were designed for? We even misuse our rational mind to the extent of providing irrational reasons. For example the person who says: 'I've failed at that once so I'll probably fail at it again' is certainly not being rational. To conclude that 'I can't' before even trying something in the absence of contrary evidence is not rational. It is as rational as the people who say they do not like a particular food or drink when they have never tasted it.

The trouble is our 'comfort zone' knows us better than anyone and hits us on our Achilles' heel. It uses reasons we find reasonable and rationale we find rational. It effectively takes our greatest aspirations and turns them into excuses for not bothering to aspire.

This comfort zone allows rationalization to take 'hold' during our conditioning years. It gave us comforting reasons for why life didn't go the way it should, for why we experienced failure. Let me illustrate.

Little nine-year-old Tommy was the only boy from his class not to be invited to a birthday party. He was very upset at first and felt affronted at being left out. Tommy started to think of reasons why he had been 'snubbed'. They had to be reasons which satisfied his honor. Suddenly he 'realized' why he hadn't been invited. Of course, he was cleverer at school than the others – that was the reason he told himself they were envious of him. This reasoning changed his feeling completely. Instead of feeling hurt about not being invited he now felt superior because he was not included.

Tommy now felt good. He had replaced his awful feeling of disappointment and humiliation with a glowing sense of pride. His mental trick had worked. What he didn't know was that he had worked the function and process of rationalization in a legitimate and valuable way – it provided a safety valve for his mental make-up. Throughout Tommy's childhood there were many such incidents and many of them were rewarding. His rationalization was a 'good friend'. As this 'good friend' that we have trained to lie for us when we needed it grows up with us it begins to get out of control and lies to us to our detriment.

When Tommy was ultimately unseated from his position at the top of the class he automatically reasoned that the boy who had replaced him had done better than he because he had the latest educational aids which Tommy's parents could not afford. As a young man Tommy 'realized' that his girl-friend had left him because another man had more money than he.

When he didn't get the job he went after, it was because he could tell the manager thought he was too good for it. Tommy grew up to be quite a happy person, of course, because he never faced up to any of his problems. He always avoided them. He never had to face any of his faults because he was able to rationalize his way around them. All his misfortunes were other people's fault.

I repeat that our rational mind and rationalization are essential to our make-up but we must ensure that it works for us and not against us. The rational mind examines and analyzes incoming messages and accepts those which are true and rejects those which are not true. Too often we confuse everything with opinions. It is our opinions and the opinions of others which we allow to affect our rational thinking. We then back up the opinions with more reasons.

For example, a person who feels fit and healthy is met by three individuals during the course of the morning. The first greeting is: 'Morning, how are you feeling today?' 'Are you alright?' 'Yes', the person replies thinking: 'Yes, I'm alright, I think, I wonder why he said that'. The second greeting is: 'Morning do you feel alright today? You don't look your usual self'. 'Don't I', replies the person and he thinks in his mind: 'Come to think of it I don't think I do feel very well now he mentions it'. The third greeting is: 'How are you today, not coming down with anything, are you?' The reply is: 'I'm not sure but I think I'll take the morning off just in case'.

The three greetings in themselves are harmless, showing friendly concern. If the man, however, values their opinions and chooses to accept them as the truth he provides reasons to be consistent with their greetings.

Controlling Rationalization

From now on be on guard against rationalization controlling you. Look out for the situations in which you detect it at once. Every time you meet up with it, resist it and you will begin to form mental patterns which will become a conditioned response opposed to the conditioned response you have had all your life. Whenever you have something to deliberate on write down all the facts relating to it. Be careful not to put down any opinions. Next, list them with the pros and cons. Go through the list and decide which are the most important points for and against the proposition, from your point of view. Examine the list to make sure you are not rationalizing. If you feel it coming on write down your 'reasons' on another sheet of paper and put it to one side. In this way you have put out your opinions and doubts. Then award each for and each against a number of points in order of merit. Add up the points in the two lists and determine the result. If you are unable to abide by the result because you are not certain what steps to take next pass it over to your super-conscious to sort out. Use your intuitive side.

Many people I know are so incredibly eloquent, funny and stimulating in casual conversation yet become almost moronic when they mount the speakers' platform. It is logical and rational that as they can interest small groups they can interest large groups, but they are muted by their 'reasoning' which they believe has come from rational thinking.

Don't let your rational thinking battle with your intuitive side by providing reasons why something can't be done. Use your rational mind to provide reasons why they can be done. Dwell upon things as possibilities and don't use the thinking process for thinking of the impossibilities. By dwelling on unfavorable outcomes your mind is occupied with worry. By dwelling on a positive outcome your mind is occupied with creative, 'how to' ideas which come to it from the intuitive side. With them working together you are on the way to finding your true purpose in life.

Finding True Purpose in Life

People often confuse goal and purpose. Goals are something we set and achieve whereas a purpose remains constant for life and is fulfilled in each moment. While goals are chosen a purpose is discovered. Everyone wonders about the purpose of life and why we are here and in the first page of this book I wrote that our purpose is to realize our potential. The true purpose of life is to find a mission and to fulfill it. To find something that absorbs us, becomes a magnificent obsession, a cause for living every day of our life, a cause that creates a sense of fulfillment, satisfaction and happiness. William Cowper said in the 18th century:

> The only true happiness comes from squandering ourselves for a purpose.

It is an unusual turn of words as there can be no waste when the cause is worthy, but I interpret his words to be a meaningful extravagance. If you can be extravagant with that which absorbs you, you are on the way to discovering your purpose.

An important key in developing your purpose is to help others. In order to help others and share our self we must become truly loving people. In this way we will determine just what our mission is.

Each of us is put on this earth to find his or her true purpose in life and it is found by following our heart's desire. Ask yourself the question: 'What difference would having a purpose in my life make?' You almost hear your mind shout at you don't you? It says: 'Everything'. Being part of a cause makes you feel good about yourself. It increases your confidence and courage. It gives the feeling that you are living for something important, worthwhile and noble. When you are aligned to your purpose you conquer all obstacles in spite of how many there are or how big they are.

Understand that you become great to the degree in which you can lose yourself in something bigger, grander and better than yourself. Where you can at the same time share yourself, your skills, talents and abilities for the benefit of others, without expecting a reward, you will set in motion the powers of universal laws. Try as you will to avoid payment for what you do in sharing and helping – blessings and rewards will be showered upon you. The more you share the more you have. Why? Your most previously valued possessions and your greatest powers are often invisible and intangible. No one can take them as only you can share them.

Earlier you wrote down a list of your chief positive qualities. You also spent some time thinking about those things that you do which really hold your attention and interest you. Start also listing actions you find nurturing the positive things you like doing most. Teaching? Learning? Sharing? Giving? Exploring? Listening? Take some time and reflect on your life. Explore the feelings that have motivated you before.

When you have done this start thinking what your purpose could be, should be. Hand it over to your super-conscious mind during your 'sittings' for ideas. Look for an answer. Consider the people you admire most. What is it you admire about them? What qualities do they embody? Think of three people you would like to emulate who are very successful individuals. Whose manner, bearing and confidence show they are relaxed within themselves. The qualities that they exude are true about you too, so write them down.

Eventually a pattern will emerge on the qualities and actions list. Begin grouping them under headings, the heading and grouping being your own, those which resonate most clearly within you. Start making sentences with the groupings keeping them short and commencing with 'I am ...'. For example: 'I am a compassionate listener', or 'I am understanding and a confident teacher' or 'I am an enthusiastic and kind sharer'. After rearranging your actions and qualities something will click. A voice inside will say: 'Yes, this is what I've always done and I enjoy doing it. I can always see myself doing it'.

This exercise forms the basis of finding your true purpose. It facilitates getting in touch with what you really are good at and what you enjoy doing. You are acting as your own mentor. As you start to get in touch with your purpose and the feeling of euphoria and commitment grows remember to keep it to yourself. Keeping your purpose to yourself is not so much secret as it is sacred. Don't let it be watered down by others who tell you that what you are doing cannot be done.

As your purpose evolves and grows your enthusiasm and courage will grow with it. You will be seen as a person who believes in yourself and is true to yourself. Respect, love and admiration for you will increase as you become associated with that true integrity, clarity and depth of character that people who know you take strength from. Your purpose may not take you to becoming a head of state or millionaire but it is guaranteed to ensure you reach your highest potential. The achievement of true integrity and well-rounded character is in itself success. As the seeds of your purpose grow into a beautiful plant keep the roots deep within yourself and let the world share in its fruits.

Practice, Practice, Practice

- As I have said, becoming a loving person to others and practicing 'do to others what you would have them do to you' is essential to finding true purpose. It will take courage and practice but the benefits are worth it.

- Practice doing your best to try and never violate your honor by lying or cheating and always accept total responsibility for everything that you are and everything that you become.

- Practice clean thoughts, speech and habits. Learn to forgive and feed your mind with loving positive thoughts.

- Practice standing up for your rights and the rights of others against undesirable influences, coaxing of friends and threats of enemies.

- Practice setting noble goals and ideals and work towards them faithfully and making the best of your opportunities.

- Practice saving money so that you can pay your own way in this world and yet be generous to those in need and give financial help and time to worthy causes.

- Practice kindness, patience and tolerance and being a friend to every man, woman and child regardless of race, color or creed.

- Practice accepting yourself unconditionally, understanding yourself and being true to yourself. Be loyal to yourself and give loyalty to all to whom loyalty is due.

Life Achievement Plan

Dr Samuel Johnson, the great 18th-century essayist, famous among other achievements for writing the first major dictionary of the English language using illustrative historical quotations, once wrote:

> *Life affords no higher pleasure than that of surmounting difficulties, passing from one step of success to another, forming new wishes and seeing them gratified.*

In Chapter 1 I defined success as the **continuous accomplishment of planned meaningful objectives**. Goals and
objectives must be continuously decided upon and set. If
you set a series of goals and reach all of them then you must
set out new higher goals for if you don't you can no longer be
successful.

When you have almost attained your goal but not quite it is
time to choose and set another. When one dream is realized,
sometimes a deeper dream reveals itself because your horizon
has expanded. As we are naturally goal-seeking organisms we
will often experience a boredom or sense of emptiness when a
goal has been reached. This happens after the initial feeling of
fulfillment and comes about from the desire to attain the goal
being satisfied. Unless one has new goals to strive towards an
individual becomes 'no longer successful'. Many seemingly
successful people have come to me complaining of a sense of
emptiness sometimes after achieving their planned goal. I
explain to them that desire is designed to 'move' us not to
maintain the status quo. There can be no standing still only
moving forward or slipping back.

That is why it is so important to discover a purpose which
you can set your goals towards. **A true purpose is never
attainable**. It constantly expands and grows as you expand
and grow. Goals aligned to your purpose may stay the same
but the quantifying factors are raised with your broadening
horizon and make you become aware of your unlimited
potential. The person who starts running to become fitter and
healthier may then set a goal to run a marathon. As it
becomes achievable new goals incorporating better times are
set. A personal best may become a country best and expand
the individual's horizon to reveal the possibility of running
for his or her country, of being sponsored internationally, of
becoming a coach of other runners, of holding training

schools, to developing other winners. Each goal achieved brings its own individual rewards and satisfaction. This 'achievement feeling' creates the habit of success and solidifies the confidence, character and belief to go on to greater dreams.

A goal to run your own company, or be top of your own company may remain intact for example, but you may look to double your salary. The goal may change entirely as you become able to invest time and money in areas which are worthwhile to you and which start revealing themselves to the 'improved you'.

As you begin to grow in the confidence that the sense of feeling of success at consistently setting and achieving goals brings, you will become aware of the changing and strengthening self-image that reflects the best you, the true you. It is important now to look further down the road to the future life you want to have.

Below is a five-year achievement plan. It differs from the goal sheet you are using for your short, medium and long-term goals in as much that it focuses on what you must do and what you must not do in order to attain what you want.

Your goal plan sheets will in turn act as a yardstick to monitor the required changes in your day-to-day life in order to create the future you want. It is important to create a clear, vivid mental picture of how you see your desired life in five years' time.

Close your eyes and go back into your 'cinema' and see yourself on the screen. What do you look like? Where are you? What are you wearing? What are you doing? Where do you work? Who is there with you? How do you feel? What does your house look like? What car do you drive? Take your time and picture as much detail as you can and let yourself feel the pleasure of having the life you want.

LIFE ACHIEVEMENT PLAN

It is five years in the future and I _____

_____

_____

_____

_____

_____

To achieve this future I will _____

_____

_____

_____

_____

To achieve this future I will avoid _____

_____

_____

_____

_____

I will commit myself to achieving this **Five-Year Plan**

Date _____ Signed _____

Next, write a description of how you see yourself and make it in the present tense as if you had already achieved it. For example: 'it is five years in the future and I ...'.

Ask yourself what must I do to make my future plan a reality? How can I learn what is required to achieve it?

What must I *avoid* doing to make any desired future a reality? List all the steps you can think of and keep adding to them as and when you think of more.

You now have a list of all the activities you must and must not do in order to attain the future you want and you can use the information for your goal plan sheets which in turn will support your life plan. Remember, everything counts and if you see yourself in five years being slim, fit and eloquent then you know you must avoid over-eating and procrastinating and start doing exercise and reading at least 15 minutes a day, something which interests and stimulates you and is aligned to the knowledge required to be the person you want to be.

Place your life achievement plan where you can see it every day and make a note in your diary every 30 days to review it. At each review make any changes and calculate your progress. This will actively motivate and stimulate you to set new higher goals each time you near one particular goal and to take the proper action to achieve your plan.

Everything You Need is Within Reach

Dr Russell Conwell founded Temple University with money he raised from giving over 6,000 lectures on a now famous story called the 'Acre of Diamonds'. It was a true story of a farmer who became so excited about tales of other farmers who had made their fortunes from discovering diamond mines that he sold his farm and spent his life unsuccessfully searching for the prize gems. Eventually impoverished, desolate and alone he took his own life.

The new owner of his farm had in the meantime discovered an attractive stone in his riverbed and placed it on his mantelpiece. A visitor inspecting the conversation piece couldn't believe what he was holding – one of the largest diamonds ever discovered. The farm that had been disposed of in order that the first farmer might find a diamond mine, actually turned out to be the most productive diamond mine on the continent. The first farmer had already owned acres of diamonds but he had sold them for practically nothing in order to look for them elsewhere.

The philosophy of this story is that diamonds, like opportunities, are disguised. Diamonds in their rough state do not look like diamonds, they require preparation. Study and preparation have to be done before opportunities can be capitalized on. All the talents, skills and abilities required for whatever you want you already own in an undeveloped and unprepared state. Everything that you require is under your own feet or at least within reach so you don't have to look elsewhere to realize your goals.

If the first farmer had taken the time to study and prepare himself, to understand what diamonds look like in their rough form and thoroughly explored where he was first before looking elsewhere, all of his dreams would have come true. Each of us is standing in his or her own acre of diamonds. Before you go running off to greener pastures make certain you have explored your own just as green pastures. If someone's pastures are greener it may simply be because they are getting better care and attention. Remember, while you are looking at the other pastures, other people are looking at yours.

Use your mind to explore thoroughly the opportunities and possibilities lying hidden in what you are presently doing before turning to something new. If what you are doing at present is from a previous choice there were probably good reasons for it. If it is not giving what you require then it is perhaps time for some further exploration.

Often people have to experience several careers to develop their potential until they find their true calling. The important thing to understand is that within every kind of work there is another opportunity waiting to be noticed. Take the time to look at what you are doing in the way that a stranger might and ask yourself: 'Why do I do that this way or that way?' Sometimes we are so close to something we do not see the opportunity right under our nose. We do not see the wood for the trees. A stranger might ask: 'Why has he not noticed how to modify or multiply what he is doing?' How often have you heard about an old established business being turned round with the same existing resources but just utilizing new ideas or approaches?

Ask yourself regularly: 'How can I improve what I am doing or increase my service today?' 'Am I missing opportunities because my methods disguise them?' 'What better ways are there of doing what I am doing?' 'Will what I do be done in the same way ten years from now?' Everything is in a state of evolution, how can I do what will eventually be done anyway?

Everything you need to learn, a new skill required to attain a goal is within your reach. Hundreds of libraries hold thousands of books containing the information to instruct you on your path. How much does it cost to join a library? Nothing, yet only a few percentage of the population are members. The other percentage are so busy finding reasons for not being able to read what they need. Countless courses are held most nights of the week teaching all types of skills. Get the information on them – there may be a course you are not even aware of. While enjoying a walk I noticed lots of varieties of fungus in the form of mushrooms and toadstools. How many of us dare to pick them to enjoy later in a meal. On routinely checking courses available I discovered not one but four field evening courses to learn how to differentiate edible and inedible fungus. Amazing? Not really, everything you need to learn is within your reach if you look for it and if the course you require doesn't exist then there lies the opportunity to start your own and learn while you teach others.

Ignorance is not bliss and what you don't know will hurt you as you are possibly standing in a diamond mine but are not proficient enough in your subject to recognize it.

Diamonds, like opportunities, do require hard work but by paying the price in hard work by becoming a specialist in your field you will reap and enjoy the benefits. The majority of people will put down your stumbling on your diamond mine as a 'bit of good luck' for that is the only way they are able to explain away their lack of opportunity.

Mine Your Opportunities and Purpose

Most people are oblivious to the fact that opportunities await recognition. To become a diamond miner you must break away from the crowd. You must stop assuming that because the majority of people live in a certain way, it is the best way. Because it is not, it's the average way. Those going the best way are so far out in front that their dust blinds the rest. They are the people who mark the way forward – who are prepared for opportunities, recognize and seize them. They don't waste their life running around looking for a pot of gold at the end of a rainbow, they employ themselves with mining their purpose using all the unlimited opportunities available to them.

List all the opportunities that surround what currently employs you. Really think about them and put down whatever comes to mind. Ask yourself, how can you increase your knowledge of what you currently do? Find out what courses, books and tapes exist in your subject. Ask how can you improve your job performance right now? If you don't ask your mind, then your mind won't give. Ask and really get the creative juices going. Most of us have been 'asking' for years but in the wrong vein – in a negative sense. For example we ask worryingly: 'What am I going to do if such and such should happen?' or: 'What if I were to lose this or that?' or: 'Not win this or that?' Our mind obligingly obeys our commands and gives us more to worry about making our imagination once again work against us and not for us. Asking how you can keep the 'wolf from the door' will at best give us ideas to keep the status quo. Asking how we can improve our performance would at worst give new, even if only mediocre ideas, designed to do just that.

Ask and expect the right answer of yourself and your mind will perform. It wants to. It has to. It's simply obeying your instructions. Look and expect to see opportunity where others don't or won't and you will see them as your mind is acting in a manner consistent with your instructions and will make you see things you overlooked before.

Making Success a Habit

In Chapter 1 I said that we were unique in the fact that we had the power of choice. We always have a choice. The trouble is, however, that many of us have delegated that choice to habits formed long ago. Habits are not an instinct they are a reaction. A reaction formed by continually doing something. We all formed habits when we knew far less about life than we know now. Unwittingly we formed habits and they then in turn form us. The habits that we allowed to form years ago end up controlling our lives today. **If we don't conquer our bad habits they will inevitably and eventually conquer us**.

A habit is a conditioned response we have programmed into ourselves by continually doing a particular action until it becomes second nature. To change a habit requires work. You have to become conscious of your habits first and see what satisfaction you derive from them before you can 'replace' them with other habits.

By following your 'desires' to improve and become what you want to become you will automatically be sowing the seeds of new positive habits which will in turn highlight your bad habits and effectively root them out by displacement. All you need to do is continually take action towards what you want and not what you don't want and your negative habits will be substituted for your positive habits.

Take, for example, a bucket of water and drop in stones one by one. The fluid representing your bad habits will eventually be displaced leaving a bucketful of positive ones. As new habits 'force' us to react in a manner consistent with what we continually do, we must continue to take action to ensure that our good habits get stronger and our bad habits disappear. The hard work, of course, is the conditioned resistance we experience in making the change. We know what to do but if we do not perceive the changes we want quickly we fall off the wagon. If for 20 years you have never spent 30 minutes a day thinking, writing and planning about what you really want and taking some action immediately towards it, but instead have spent the same time just thinking about what you don't want, expecting the worse and hoping for the best, then after a while you forget the 'new ways of thinking' and go back to your old comfortable way even if it is leading you to mediocrity.

Only by persistently and consistently taking action over and over again will you build up the habit for goal-setting. Working on goal-setting in the way I have shown you will automatically bring lots of little successes. Everything you do is measured, achieved and rewarded. The procedure of lots and lots of successes not only builds your confidence, self-esteem and self-worth but it actually creates the habit of success, physically, mentally and emotionally. As habits eventually form us, you will inevitably be a habitual success.

Of course, it takes some degree of discipline in building new habits but by building up the habit of success by achieving numerous accomplishments which in turn are chunked down in their steps of accomplishment, the discipline required becomes easy. As long as the goals you want to take are realistic yet challenging your desire will strengthen your discipline through your determination. The old saying that discipline weighs ounces and regret weighs tons is true. When you have something to do, when you know it is right for you and must be done, chunk it into bite size yet challenging goals. Please don't say: 'I must get down to doing that sometime'; start forming the habit of doing what you must do by doing it every day. That is how you form the habit of doing 95 percent of what you do now in the first place! Use the 'reaction' process based on repetition for your benefit and not for your detriment.

Repetition – the Mother of Learning

What I have shared with you in this chapter does require action. 'Going into the silence' is one of the most valuable things you will learn. To know is not enough. Knowing is passive, experiencing is active. There will inevitably be difficulties for some in finding their own space to 'listen for ideas'.

You may not be able to do it every day to constant distractions. It is important that you schedule in your weekly life time to think, listen, contemplate, write your goals, make your plans and review your progress. You will find in time that you are getting more done in less time. You will find that you understand your wants and desires better and can interpret your thoughts and ideas more easily each time you crystallize them in writing. Only by constant repetitive action do the talents you require become smooth enough for you to carry out tasks without even having to organize yourself as you would have had to organize yourself when you first started making changes in your life. Repetition turns imperceptible improvements into grandiose ones. Only you can do that. Reading this book will not change your life, just as reading a guide book to France will not show you France. It may give you a sense of France, perhaps, but France is France and can only be experienced through action. This book has been written to give you a sense of what you are capable of achieving, to increase your awareness of being aware and understanding of how you can release your unlimited potential. Please don't deny yourself by not taking definite concerted action. Once you have the momentum you will become unstoppable. Consistency creates momentum and momentum is sustained through consistency.

> Nothing is impossible when we follow our inner guidance
>
> *G. Jampolsky*
>
> *and*
>
> The more confident we are the more
> intuition works through us.
>
> *P. Neary*
>
> *and*
>
> I never came upon any of my discoveries
> through the process of rational thinking.
>
> *A. Einstein*
>
> You are here for a purpose. There is no duplicate
> of you in the whole wide world. There never
> has been. There never will be. You were brought
> here to fill a certain need. Take time to think that over.
>
> *L. Austin*

THOUGHTS FOR SOWING

1. Take time for 'quiet time' and you will have more time *because* of that 'guide time'.

2. The more you are prepared to trust yourself and follow your inner guidance, the more you will have. Your purpose is to *be* yourself and *do* what you really love.

3. Look for the opportunity in your own 'garden'. The grass may look greener elsewhere, but it will have been just as hard to cut.

4. Don't waste time 'reasoning why you can't', instead intuitively find out how you can.

5. Practice, practice, practice. A little every day makes everything count towards the habit of success.

Chapter 7

Releasing Your Unlimited Potential

We live in an age where change is considered a necessary pre-requisite for growth more than at any previous period in history. It is an age where people are increasingly becoming aware of being aware, and of what they want. Indeed, people are today conscious of themselves as being powerful thinking individuals with the capabilities to achieve anything they set their mind on.

Using the information within this book you have the opportunity to start drawing on an inexhaustible supply of potential within your own being. Your belief in the wealth of human potential is an obvious requirement but by applying the proven principles to activate your hidden strength, your beliefs will quickly build. Why? Because of the results. For your part all you simply have to do is apply them continually by first giving to yourself, working on yourself, fulfilling your goals and dreams. Next, when you are enjoying the abundance of your dreams and filled to overflow you *don't* hoard it, you give it to others.

By giving what abilities and talents you have and want to develop to others you will receive even more. One gives of what one is. Whatever ability one has developed in whatever area one has developed it, is shared. One of the great open gifts of life is that giving to others gives us more than we give away. When you do this and discover the results there is no stopping you.

The moment you understand the fact that you can rise, you *will* rise and you will have absolutely no limitations other than those you set yourself.

In recognizing yourself for what you are you realize that 'environment' will never condition you again but that you will always condition your environment. You will not have to leave a particular environment where you work as the force you carry and exude will affect and change matters so that you create new conditions in the old environment.

As you begin to grow in confidence and the realization of how you control you, negative influences will weaken and disappear with a rapidity directly in proportion to the extent of your realization.

The more you are yourself the stronger you will become. To be oneself is the *only* worthy and satisfactory person to be. Don't surrender your individuality to the conformity of life that restricts the growth of your individual spirit. By preserving your uniqueness you will create a better set of conditions in your world not available to the person who has surrendered their identity on the false belief of more security. People who are not true to themselves become even more insecure and lost.

If you live your life to suit others you will *never* suit them and the more you try the more unreasonable and exacting they will become. To be yourself, study yourself. Study yourself not only from the point of what you are but also of what you may become. This will assist you in improving the qualities you want to. By continually practicing right thinking the negative emotions will continue to lose their power over you.

Remember always that every bad habit will lead you away from what you want. The world owes you nothing – except the chance. This is your chance to break the hold certain habits have on you. Become aware of them. Resolve to break them. The crucial step that makes all the difference must be your own. You and only you must initiate action for it to be permanent. Discipline yourself to talk only positively never negatively. Too many of us spend more time criticizing ourselves and others than we do praising and more time remembering what we did wrong instead of what we did right. Look for the good and not the bad. How would you like to spend your life doing good and then be remembered for one human indiscretion which marred it? No one has the right to mar another person's life. A particular performance may be constructively criticized but on what basis have we the right to be judgmental? Is any one of us holier than thou? Yet it is done and this negative type of thinking becomes a habit effectively weakening us from our own source of potential.

We all know people who almost have a compulsion to point out the one small error in what they have just witnessed, whatever it may be. They genuinely believe that they are being useful – it is a habit they are unaware of. I guarantee that if you only give more praise than criticism people will most assuredly come back for more. Why? Because our craving for 'being counted for something' is enormous. Remember this when you next criticize yourself! Stop it! Start congratulating yourself for being the unique person you are.

From Right Now

From this moment on I want you to see yourself as you really want to be: prosperous, optimistic, living, caring, giving and respected. Change the habit of seeing yourself as someone who can accomplish nothing spectacular. Don't wish. Do something, because action is necessary no matter what habit you desire to change.

Remember to establish your values. Take time to know what you stand for. If you don't you will fall for anything. Keep asking yourself what you stand for until the answer manifests itself. As with your goals write them down. Crystallize your thinking on paper. Stick to your mental diet for 30 days in order to focus your goals and know what you really want. Please don't cheat yourself with this. Of course, it is hard work initially only because you are not used to the type of thinking it involves. Trust me on this and please keep doing it as the results you enjoy will make you stand out from the crowd.

Results in the form of changes may be imperceptible at first but over the period of your lifetime plan will be enormous. If you just improve by 1 per cent a week in a five-year period you will have improved by 250 per cent! Remember this next time you meet someone who has not seen you for several months. They will notice a huge change in you.

As you inevitably become aware of your rapid growth in understanding, the immutable laws which control the universe become more available to you. More about the laws in a while, but understand that any power that is possible for one human soul is possible for another. The same laws operate in every life. We can be men and women of power or men and women of impotence. Whatever estimate you put on yourself will determine the effectiveness of your work along any line. The limitations you choose to set for yourself will always hold you back. When, however, you come into the realization of your oneness with the infinite life and power of the universal mind and open yourself that it may work through you, you will find that you have entered upon an entirely new phase of life.

How Tall Does a Tree Grow?

It is the nature of man to compartmentalize as much as he can and pigeonhole and label everything. Goals must be measurable in order to be challenging yet realistic. I am often asked, however, how much one should do of something to improve.

I believe that we are here to develop our potential. As our potential is unlimited we must do as much as we can. If you want to know how many books to read, read as many as you can. The one that you miss isn't any good to you is it?

Always extend yourself to your full capacity. Do the very best you can. A simple rule is just to not call 'enough' an amount, but call it the very best.

If a person is doing the very best they can and earning $30,000 a year you can say they are earning enough as they are doing the very best they can. If however a person is capable of earning $100,000 per annum but is only earning $30,000 per annum you can call them a loser because they are abusing their abilities. The amount is not important, what is important is to extend yourself to the full capacity of your reach.

How much should you do? As much as you can. In the garden of your life if you rest too long weeds will take over. 'Whatever your hands find to do, do it with all your might'. How much should you learn? As much as you can. The ant philosophy again teaches us what to do. How much work do ants do? As much as they can. How much food do they gather? As much as they can.

Doing less than you know you can do causes all kind of guilt feelings manifesting themselves in certain ways. When people feel they have not done their best they feel they have cheated themselves – they certainly haven't been true to themselves – and they start to rationalize why they didn't perform as they know they were capable of. This leads to a shift in personal responsibility to blaming external circumstances and opens the door wider for negative thinking to take control of the individual.

When you are involved in what you want to do, however, your work becomes a 'labor of love' and you enjoy a wonderful sense of satisfaction when you have completed your work. Only when you do the best you can do, you discover that you are capable of doing more.

How much of a person do you want to become? As much of a person as you can. Nature allows a tree to grow as tall as it can. A tree doesn't just stop growing half way up because it hasn't got the power of choice. Unless it is pruned to grow a certain height it is natural for it to grow as high as it can.

Our previous choices due to a previous conditioning has created a regular pruning of our own growth. Choose now to be the very best you can in everything that counts in the growth of the new you. In that way you will grow as much as you can. As you do you will enjoy what you do even more. The words of J.W. Von Goethe are again appropriate:

Are you in earnest, then seize this very minute.
Whatever you can do, or dream you can, begin it.
Boldness has genius, power and magic in it.
Only engage and the mind grows heated.
Begin, and then the work will be completed.

The minute you start extending yourself is the moment you value yourself. It's not what you achieve – it's what you become.

Self-reliance Above All

To know yourself, understand yourself, is to begin to trust yourself. When you begin to have confidence in your own feelings and act on them you are becoming self-reliant. When you are self-reliant and enjoy this self-trust you no longer worry what others say about you because you are your own person.

To paraphrase Emerson, whosoever would be somebody, must be a non-conformist. Society, however, requests, even demands, that we conform to its particular way of thinking. And to what cost do we surrender our individual character by imitating and thus being conditioned by society, which acts in the name of its 'knowing best' for the individual? What you must do is all that concerns you and not what people think. It is hard because you will find the world full of those who think they know what is your duty better than you know it. It is easy in the world to live after the world's opinion and it is easy in solitude to live after our own; but the individual is the person who, in the midst of the crowd, can still keep the independence of solitude.

Each time you conform to the opinion of others you blur the impressions of your own character. All the shoulds and shouldn'ts of conformity repress the individual's feelings of what is right for them as an individual. Each person is their own cause and should know their own worth and not be timid and apologetic for following their own path or being afraid to say 'I think' or 'I am'. So often we dismiss our own brilliant ideas and thoughts, simply because they are our own, and in turn favor the expression of society. And from wherever does society gain the expression? From a past non-conformist individual who is no longer alive to threaten the status quo.

All great individuals who follow their own hearts are always initially misunderstood, even maligned. But only initially. People who act on their own account, following their own intuition and not just the intuition of others, inevitably stand out from the crowd. He or she finds all the doors open. All eyes follow with desire. Society solicitously and apologetically celebrates the individual because he or she kept to the path and ignored the disapproving comments.

Society listens and agrees with the 'rightful' disheartened person it has spawned, when that person is unable to get a 'rightful' position after their studies. It seems understandable to society and friends that he or she should complain and therefore be provided with a comforting ear. Another who believes: 'if it's going to be, it's up to me' does whatever it takes. Not waiting for the world to do something, they become the center of their own universe and create opportunity after opportunity. They never imitate knowing that that which they can do best, none but their maker can teach them. People advance and improve through belief in themselves and their abilities. Society never advances. It cannot. It changes continually acquiring new rules and losing old ones. It doesn't like self-reliance with its realities, creators and individual thinking. In its place it prefers names and customs, badges of office and dead institutions. Society is a wave which moves forward with different water at each crest because the people who make up a nation today eventually die and their experience dies with them.

Is it so bad to be misunderstood? To be great is to be misunderstood. Every individual who left his or her mark was misunderstood before being applauded. Why? Simply because they did their own thing. They were guided by what was right for them and not what was right for society.

Start to become aware of the forced smile which you put on in company where you do not feel at ease, in answer to conversation which does not interest you. The unspontaneous muscles which become uncomfortable to you are the physical discomfort which you experience by being what you feel you should be. The inner sensation you experience dissipates your inner energy which is strong only when you are you.

Don't Be Distracted

Always trust in yourself and your own judgement as no one knows better than you how you feel about what you are and what you want to achieve. Let your true feelings guide you on the path that providence has planned for you.

Let go of distractions, they do not bring satisfaction. Doing things to suit others will only consume your energy and time.

See yourself walking along a path to your dream, to what you have been born for. The way is clear and your goal is in sight. All you have to do is to keep on walking. All along the way, however, there are distractions designed to test you – to see if you really want what you want, to see if you are really following your own heart, to see if you are worthy of whatever it is.

These distractions can do anything they want to tempt you from being the individual you have planned to be, to tempt you off your path – offers of food, sex, fame, power, success in any area not part of your dream, recognition, easy money, literally anything. What they cannot do, however, is get onto your path and stop you, all they can do is distract you onto theirs.

Leaving the path is always your choice. If you choose to pursue what you want and follow your path then become self-reliant about all. Trust in yourself. Don't look to a change in government, a rise in rents, a reduction in interest rates, as a sign that good days are preparing for you.

Trust and believe in yourself – great men and women have always done so. Your genuine actions speak for themselves, your conformity says nothing.

Be yourself and you will be respected for it. You will be remembered for it.

Universal Laws

You have come almost to the end of the seventh and last chapter. You could say you have reached the seventh chapter on your understanding of you, chapter being a period of your life and seven a powerful universal number of unity. The universe is in a perfectly maintained balance where the sevenfold nature of phenomena is observable everywhere. There are seven notes of music, seven colors in the visible spectrum even seven main atomic groups. The seventh wave is alleged to be the largest of its series because of the fact that it gathers up the backwash of the previous six waves. There are seven ages of man, seven heavens or seven mental states of progression. There are seven continents, seven seas, seven deadly sins, seven pillars of wisdom, seven days in the week, seven graces, seven sections to the Lord's prayer. The Pharoah saw seven kine and seven ears of corn, there were seven priests with seven trumpets marching round Jericho for seven days and on the seventh day marched round seven times and blew their trumpets seven times. In the Apocalypse we have seven churches of Asia, seven candlesticks, seven plagues. Out of the east comes the accepted teaching of seven mind centers or chakras of man. All this indicates that the universe is based on a reality of laws which even mathematics, though it shows the nature of this reality in numbers, can never explain. Whenever the universal laws are followed there is always a maintained balance. Chaos comes when we do not harmonize with the 'sevenfold nature' of the universal laws by refusing to understand, be ourselves and follow a path which we feel at one with.

It is a well-known fact that the decimal expression of seven parts of unity are as follows:

- One seventh   = 0.142857
- Two-sevenths   = 0.285714
- Three-sevenths = 0.428571
- Four-sevenths   = 0.571428
- Five-sevenths   = 0.714285
- Six-sevenths   = 0.857142

The whole of the six figures recurring.

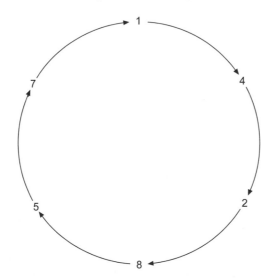

Note that the same numbers recur in the same order throughout, and that each decimal is recurring at the sixth digit. Now, there is a way in which the whole of the above expression can be set out satisfactorily in a form of a wheel of life as illustrated.

Observe that no matter at which point one starts, the completion is a matter, not of seconds, not of years, nor even of centuries, but of eternity. You have a perfect mathematical symbol of perpetual motion or infinite progression, always drawing nearer to unity but never achieving its expression. My reason for explaining the above as I have done is to impress upon you that you are inextricably linked to the universe through creation and as such are influenced by its invisible laws. You are the glass of water that has the same composition as the ocean. You are one and the same and ignorance of the laws or their existence will not release you from their influence. If you are at one with them they work with you, if you are not they work against you. They are impartial, they are immutable as the effects of the law of gravity on you. Obedience precedes authority, however, and as soon as the laws are obeyed the laws do our bidding. In the same way the laws of electricity must be obeyed before the power of electricity is at our disposal. If we misunderstand or misapply the laws of electricity, then disaster is inevitable. So it is with the laws of the universal mind.

Maintained Balance

Whichever way you turn the mathematical expression above, it balances itself. Universal laws act to maintain the balance. The laws of sowing and reaping, cause and effect, action and reaction, correspondence and compensation have different names and terminology expounded by their various authors from Jesus to Plato, Newton to Emerson but they all refer to the iron principle of what you put out you get back. In the east the law is known as the law of Karma meaning in the Sanskrit the law of 'come back'. Whatever you send out in thought, word or deed will return to you again. How else can balance be maintained? Life is no game of chance, as it is often believed, it is like a boomerang that always comes back to the hand that threw it.

Whatever you 'give out' you will receive back. That is why it is so important to keep your thoughts on what you want and not what you don't want. Your outer world will manifest itself because of your inner world. This book's purpose is to get you to put yourself in order first. What you want will come to you if you act in a way to prepare for it.

A Living Magnet

The person who lives in the understanding and acceptance of their oneness with this infinite power becomes a magnet, attracting to themselves a continual supply of whatsoever they desire.

If one holds thoughts of poverty, of not paying bills or losing your job, home or health, then the chances are that the thoughts will themselves attract the situations almost like self-fulfilling prophesies. Conversely, if we think abundance we will have abundance. You have to see yourself receiving before you receive. You can control any situation if at first you control yourself. When you control your thinking you effectively determine the feelings that make you act in the way you do. Pythagoras thought that the more you understand the universe the more you acknowledge that everything that exists is a vibration. Thoughts we send out couple with similar frequencies. Set positive vibratory forces into operation and you will effectively be placing a magnet that will draw the situations, conditions, people and circumstances in harmony with those thoughts. By working on yourself to constantly improve you will begin to recognize that working in and through you is the same infinite power that creates and governs all things in the universe. Sending out your thoughts can be likened to placing an advertisement in the 'situations wanted' column of a universal newspaper which has unlimited circulation. This advertisement placed in the right way, with belief, expectation, visualization and affirmation is far more effective than any printed advertisement.

A gentleman came up to me after one of my seminars and said that money and prosperity were the root of all evil in the world. He added that a person is closest to the creator with poverty. I asked him on what basis did the idea of godliness and poverty exist? There is absolutely no basis for its existence and the sooner we get away from these 'conditioned' ideas the better. Its origin comes from those who had a distorted and one-sided view of life. To quote Ralph Waldo Trine:

> True godliness is in a sense the same as true wisdom. The one who is truly wise and who uses the forces and powers with which he is endowed, to him the great universe always opens her treasure house.

Furthermore, money is not the root of evil. Love of money is the root of all evil. Money must be looked upon as a form of energy. Similar to all energies the more you give out the more you receive back. When you hoard and store it you are repressing energy. Repressing energies or 'hoarding' always brings a loss in one form or another. Using wisely brings an ever renewing gain. Opulence is the law of the universe, an abundant supply for every need if nothing is put in the way of its coming.

Life's Challenge

Each of us was born to succeed not to fail and universal laws have been designed to make it 'simple' for us. It is only through our own non-compliance that we cause our own difficulties. Conditioned beliefs have provided our own limitations to the prosperity available to all of us. Use the philosophies in this book, which are worth their weight in gold, to unblock the channels of goodness, vitality, prosperity and love waiting to flow into you. A beautiful garden remains beautiful only if it is continually tended with love and attention.

Read this book regularly and highlight those sentences or parts that have an effect on you. Practice your self-improvement continually even after it becomes second nature. As in the garden, weeds will continually attempt to grow from seeds that inadvertently land on its soil. Root out your negative thinking. Stop being influenced by what happened in the past. You are today the sum total of everything that you have ever thought. Start today to accept Life's exciting challenge. Accept it knowing you can be, have, or do anything that you really want to become, have or do.

When you commit yourself to living the life you want, providence assists in achieving your destiny. It cannot deny you. The universal laws cannot deny you. Welcome all adversity as another strengthening step on the path to your greatness. Always look for the opportunity which is simply awaiting your recognition. When the fruit in the garden is ripe it is easy to swallow and you in turn will not see things that stare you in the face, until the time arrives when the mind is ripened even though they are there for you all the time.

Always seek to improve yourself and the world you want will swiftly follow. Understand that a true symphony of success in every area of your life is deep within you, awaiting your conducting. Take charge of your life right now! Believe in yourself, your individuality and purpose. Do not go to your grave with your music still in you.

Dare to live the life that you have dreamed for yourself. Yes there is a risk. How otherwise can life be measured. But the greater risk is to neglect your potential and not do the work that only you can do. To live and not risk is not to be born.

This philosophy that I commend to you comes from experiencing the knowledge I have learned from many great sages, leaders and entrepreneurs spanning thousands of years. All knowledge already exists waiting to be discovered or more importantly re-discovered. Such ideas and principles have been my inspiration to produce tools which if used will lead you to power, to prosperity, to happiness and love while directing you to find your true purpose so long as you follow the laws and dare to be yourself.

Dare to do right, dare to be true.
You have a purpose that no other can do.
Do it so bravely, so kindly, so well,
Truth will hasten the story to tell.
Dare to be right, dare to be true.
Another's failures can never save you.
Stand by your conscience and always believe
That above all in Life you were born to succeed.
                                                                Anon

A human being is part of the whole Universe.
A. Einstein

and

All things come out of the one and
the one out of all things.
Heraclitus

so

If one advances confidently in the direction of
their dreams and endeavours to live the life they have imagined
they will meet with success . . .
You were born to succeed not to fail.
H.D. Thoreau

THOUGHTS FOR SOWING

1. In recognizing yourself for what you are, you realize that 'environment' will never condition you again, but you will always condition your environment.

2. As soon as you understand the fact you can rise, you *will* rise.

3. Always see yourself as the person you really want to be. Break down the habit of seeing yourself as someone who can accomplish nothing spectacular. Don't wish. Do something.

4. Distractions cannot get onto your path, they can only persuade you onto theirs.

5. Always seek to improve yourself and the world you want will swiftly follow. Start today to accept Life's challenge.

Index

About TEXERE

TEXERE seeks to become the most progressive and authoritative voice in business publishing by cultivating and enhancing ideas that will illuminate the global business landscape. Our name defines the spirit of our vision: TEXERE is the ancient Latin verb 'to weave.' In an increasingly global business community, we seek to create an intersection where authors and readers can share the best thinking and the latest ideas. We want to leverage the expertise and insights of leading thinkers by weaving them with TEXERE's capability to deliver them to the marketplace.

To learn more and become a part of our community visit us at:

www.etexere.com

and

www.etexere.co.uk

About the Typeface

This book was set in 11/15 Melior. The typeface was designed by Hermann Zapf, whose aim was to create a typeface ideally suited to newspapers and other applications where legibility was critical. It was released by the Stempel foundry (Frankfurt, Germany) in 1952.

About the Author

Colin Turner is Professor of Entrepreneurship and Director of the Centre of Entrepreneurial Leadership at Theseus International Management Institute, Sophia Antipolis in France, Europe's Silicon Valley. Referred to by *Business Age* as 'Europe's foremost teacher for business success,' Professor Turner's business books have sold over one million copies and are published in 25 languages. *Time Magazine* called him a 'leading authority on success, business, management and lifestyle' and his inspirational keynote lectures and groundbreaking executive workshops make him a sought after conference speaker. Professor Turner advises leading global organizations and has personally developed several multi-million dollar entrepreneurial enterprises from start-up. He can be visited at www.colinturner.com or contracted at turner@theseus.fr

About Theseus

The Theseus MBA is ranked No. 2 worldwide for Information Technology and No. 3 worldwide for e-business by '*Which MBA?*' published by the Economist Intelligence Unit, 2001. *Financial Times* MBA Survey 2001 ranked Theseus in the top ten business schools in continental Europe. Theseus operates a one-year full-time MBA focused on High-Tech Management and Entrepreneurship; a two-year part-time Executive MBA in partnership with the Anderson School at UCLA; Executive and Action Learning Programs, including developing and sustaining entrepreneurial behavior in established organizations; and applied research. A member of the World Internet Research Project, Theseus is committed to redefining management for the information age with a vision to become the most important management institute, not by size, but by impact. For further details visit www.theseus.edu or call +33 (0)4 9294 5100.

The Succeed Trilogy

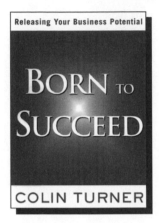

Releasing Your Business Potential

BORN TO **SUCCEED**

COLIN TURNER

Takes the reader on a journey of self-development and self-awareness.

ISBN: 1-58799-123-3
$14.95 / £8.99 / CAN$22.95

Developing Entrepreneurial Thinking

PATHS TO **SUCCEED**

COLIN TURNER

Guides the reader in developing techniques to ensure the alignment of their own personal mission with what they do professionally.

ISBN: 1-58799-125-X
$14.95 / £8.99 / CAN$22.95

Creating Entrepreneurial Organizations

LEAD TO **SUCCEED**

COLIN TURNER

How to develop the ideas and philosophy captured in the first two books, and apply them to established organizational structures.

ISBN: 1-58799-124-1
$14.95 / £8.99 / CAN$22.95